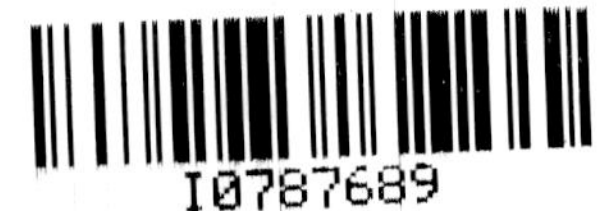

Edited by Sabrine Micha Na
Layout by Vagner Lopes
Photographs by Ardana.artwork

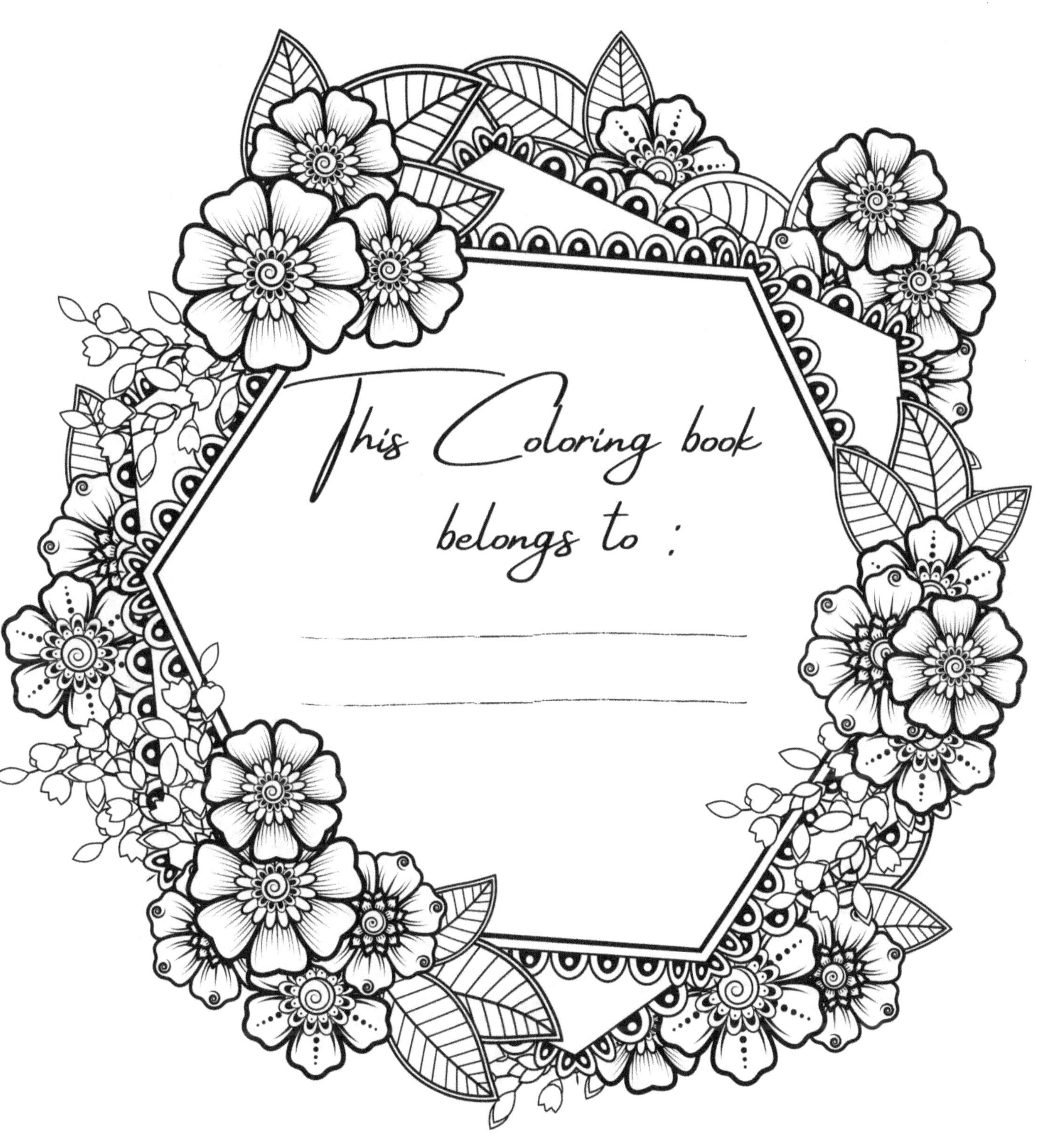

This Coloring book
belongs to :

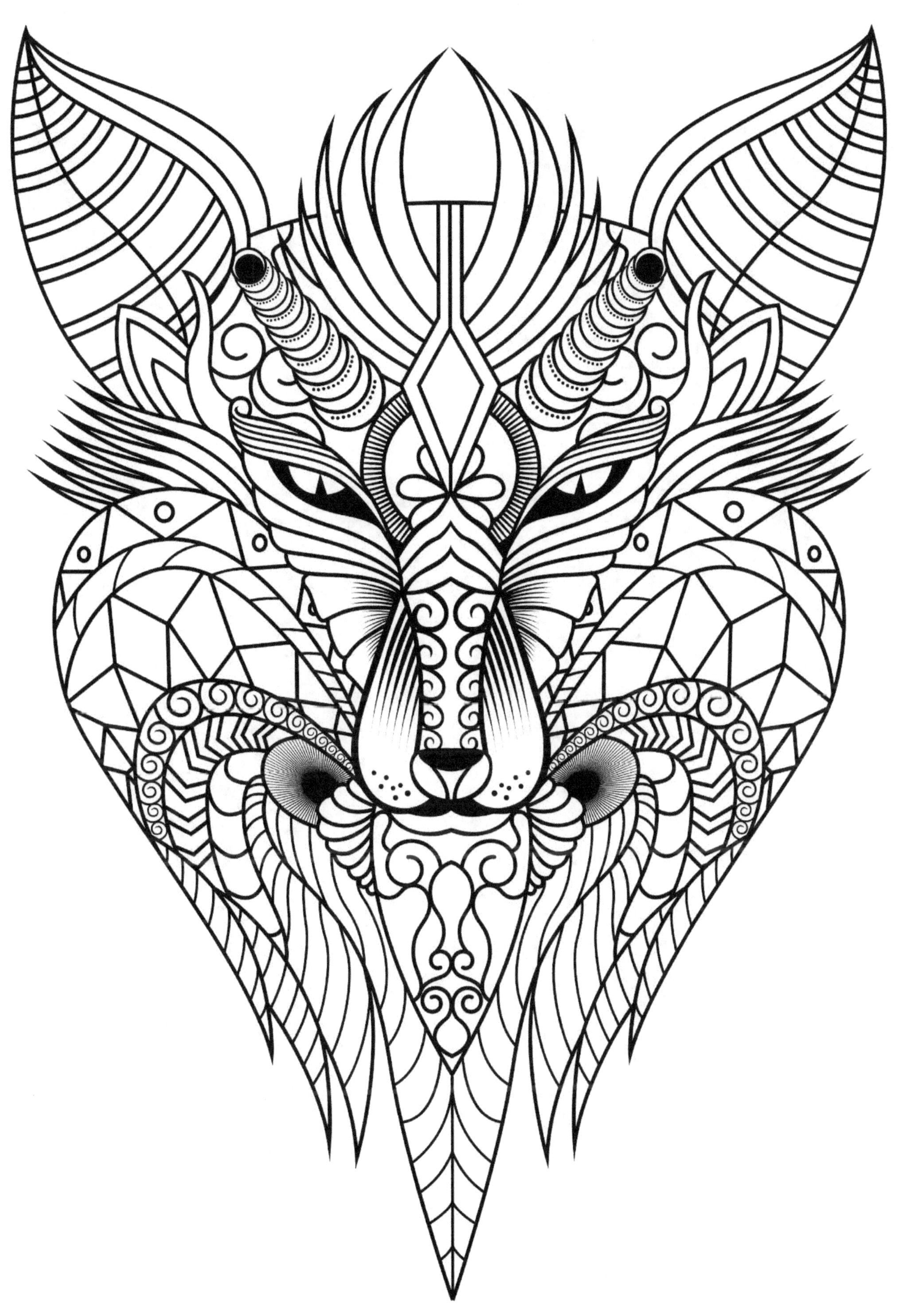

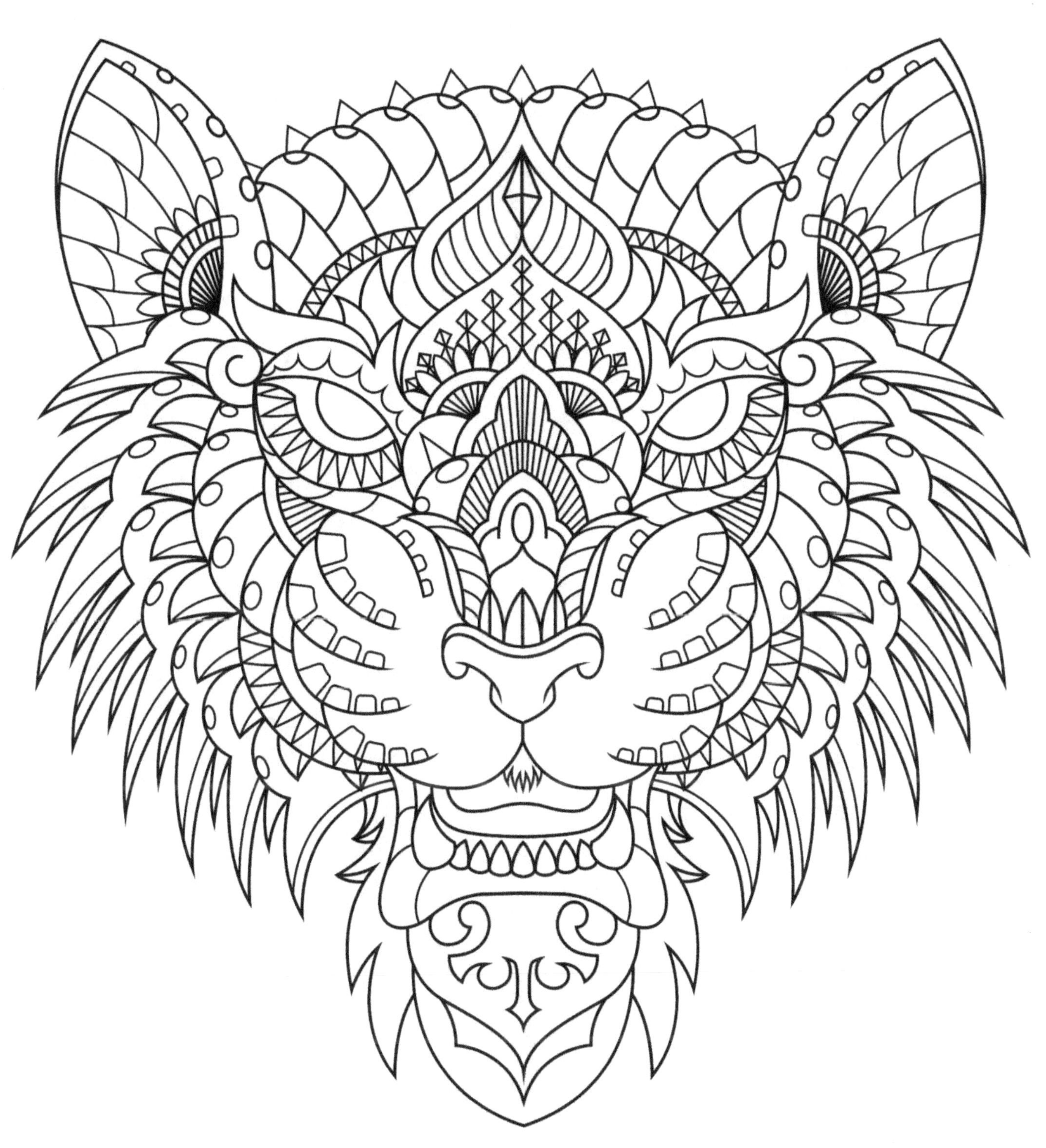

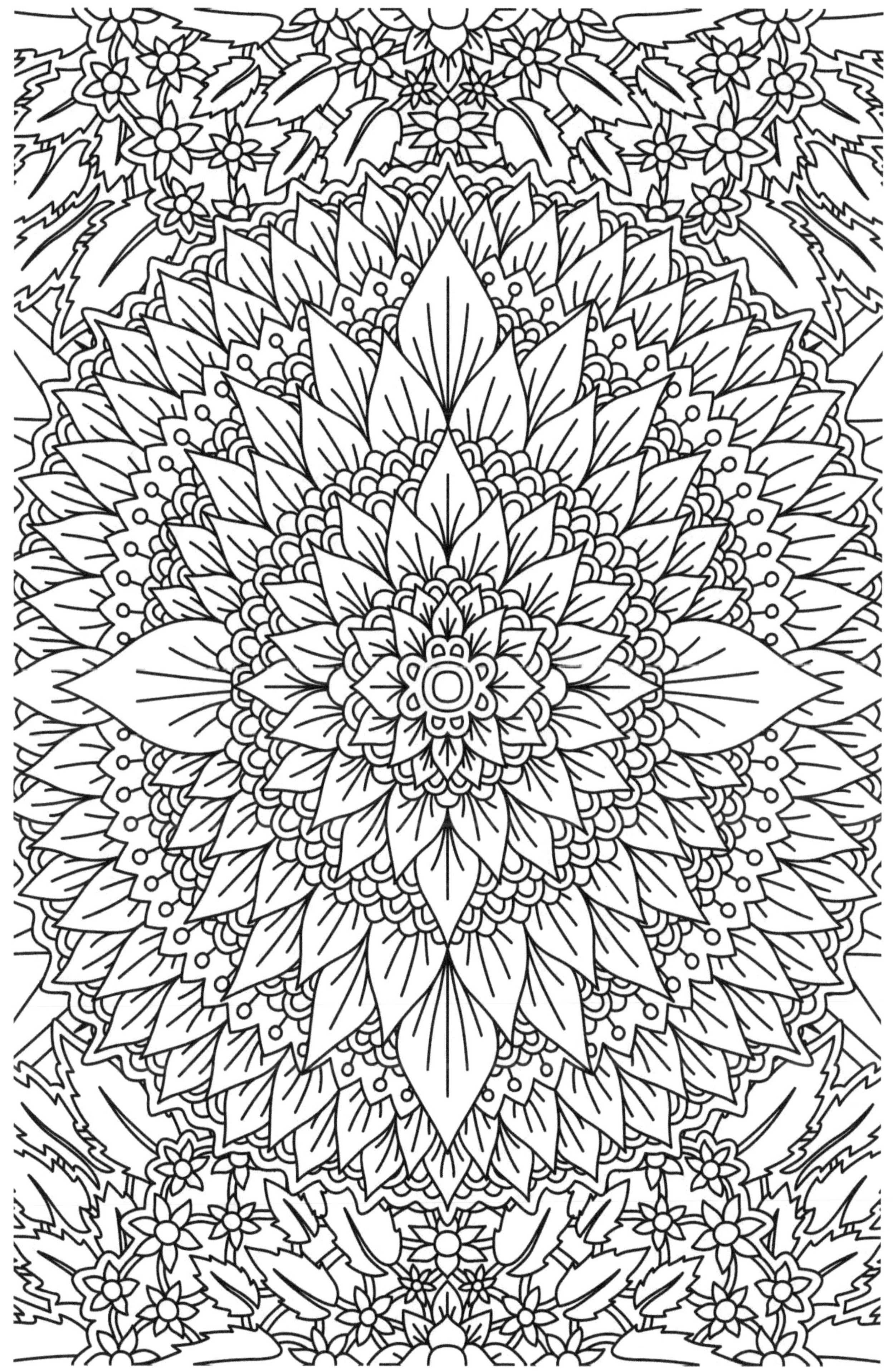

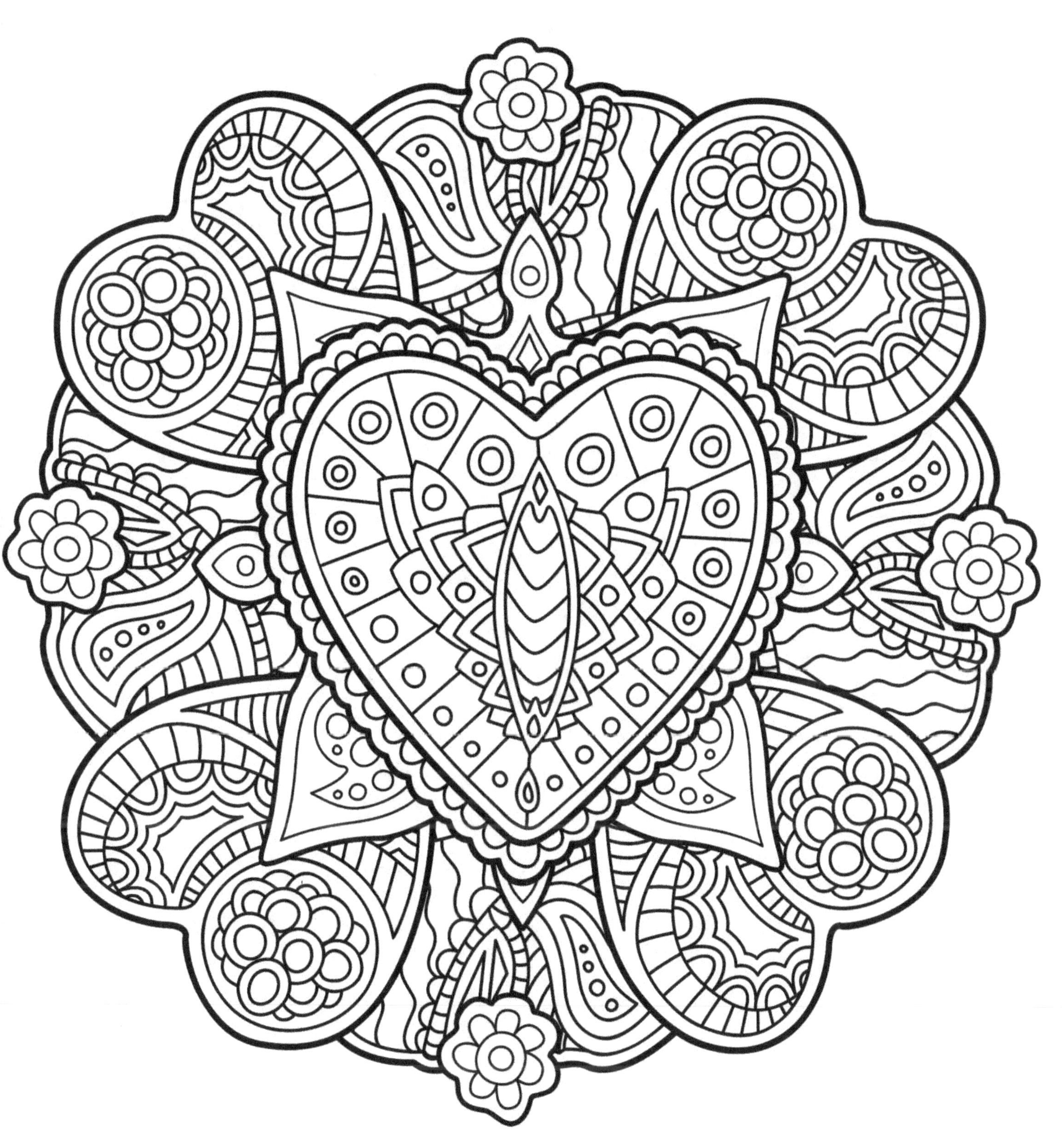

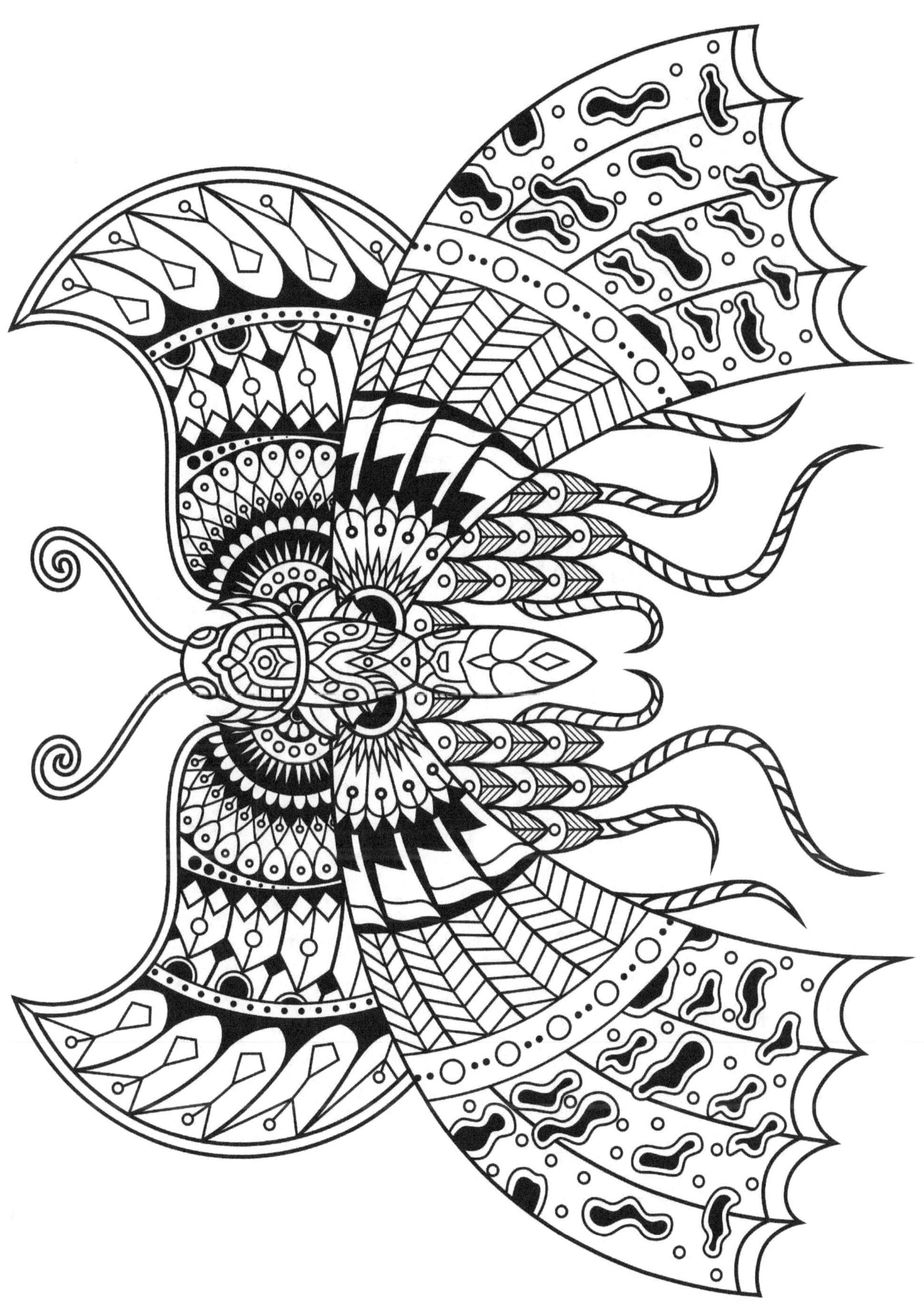

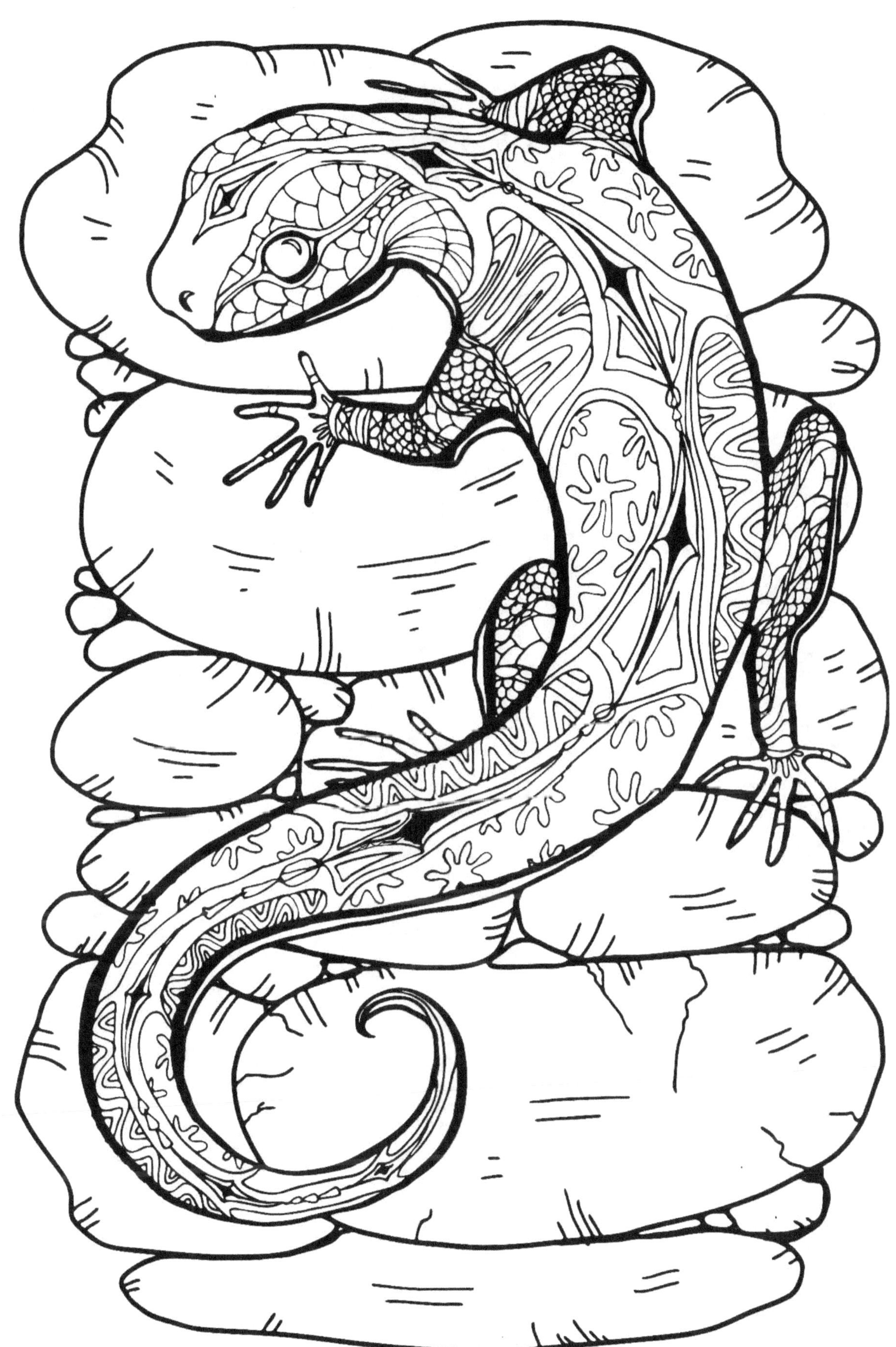

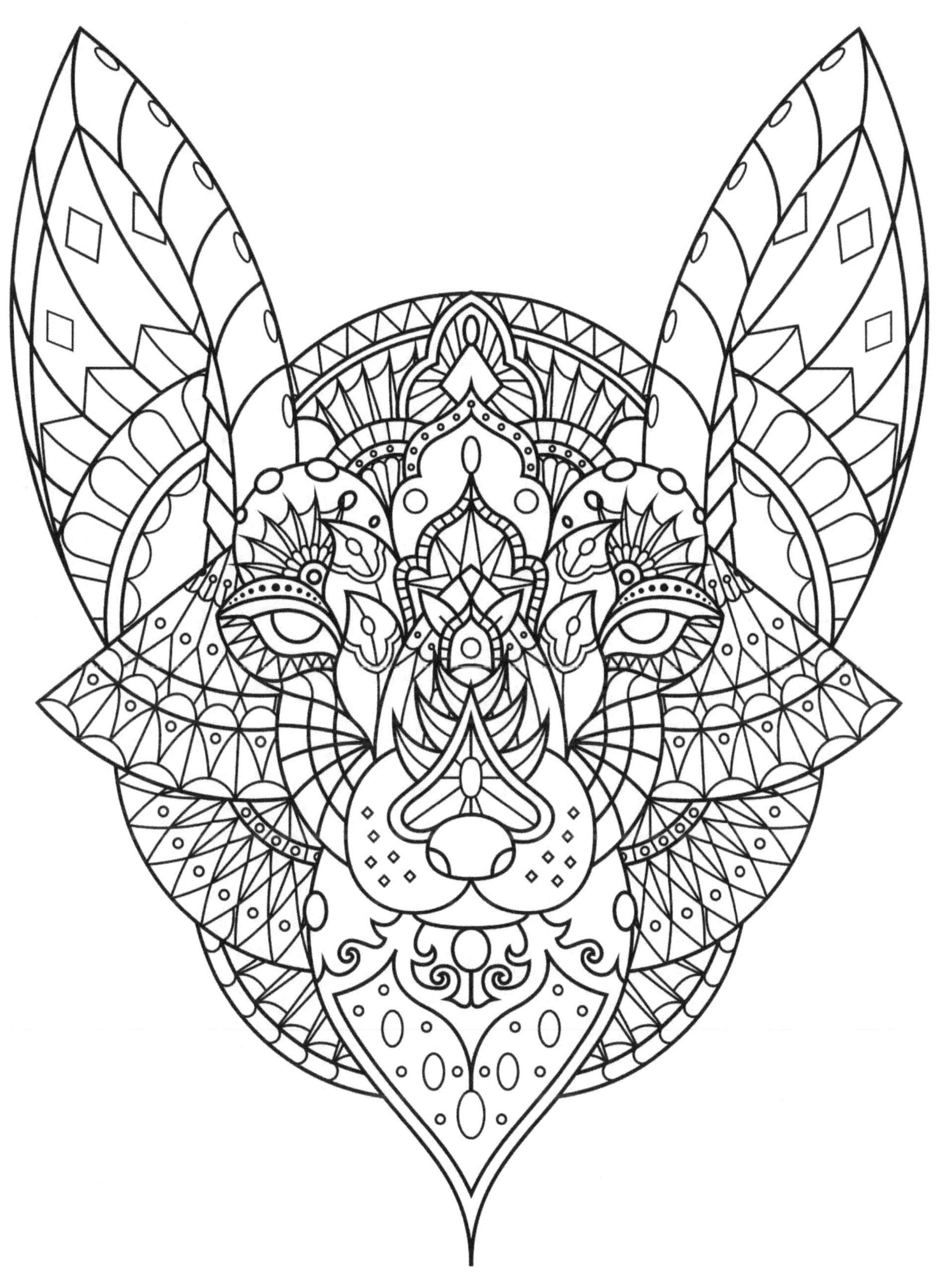

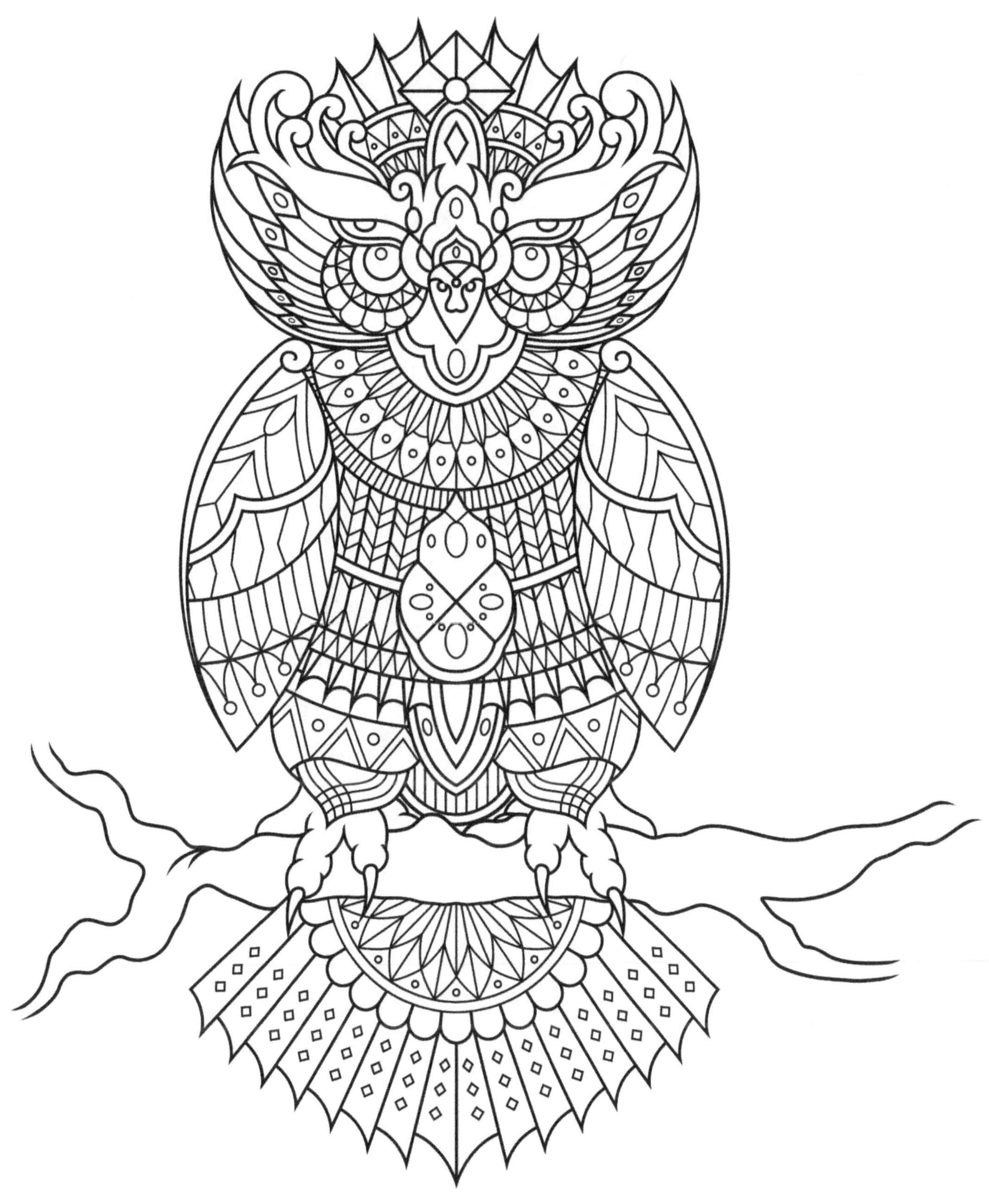

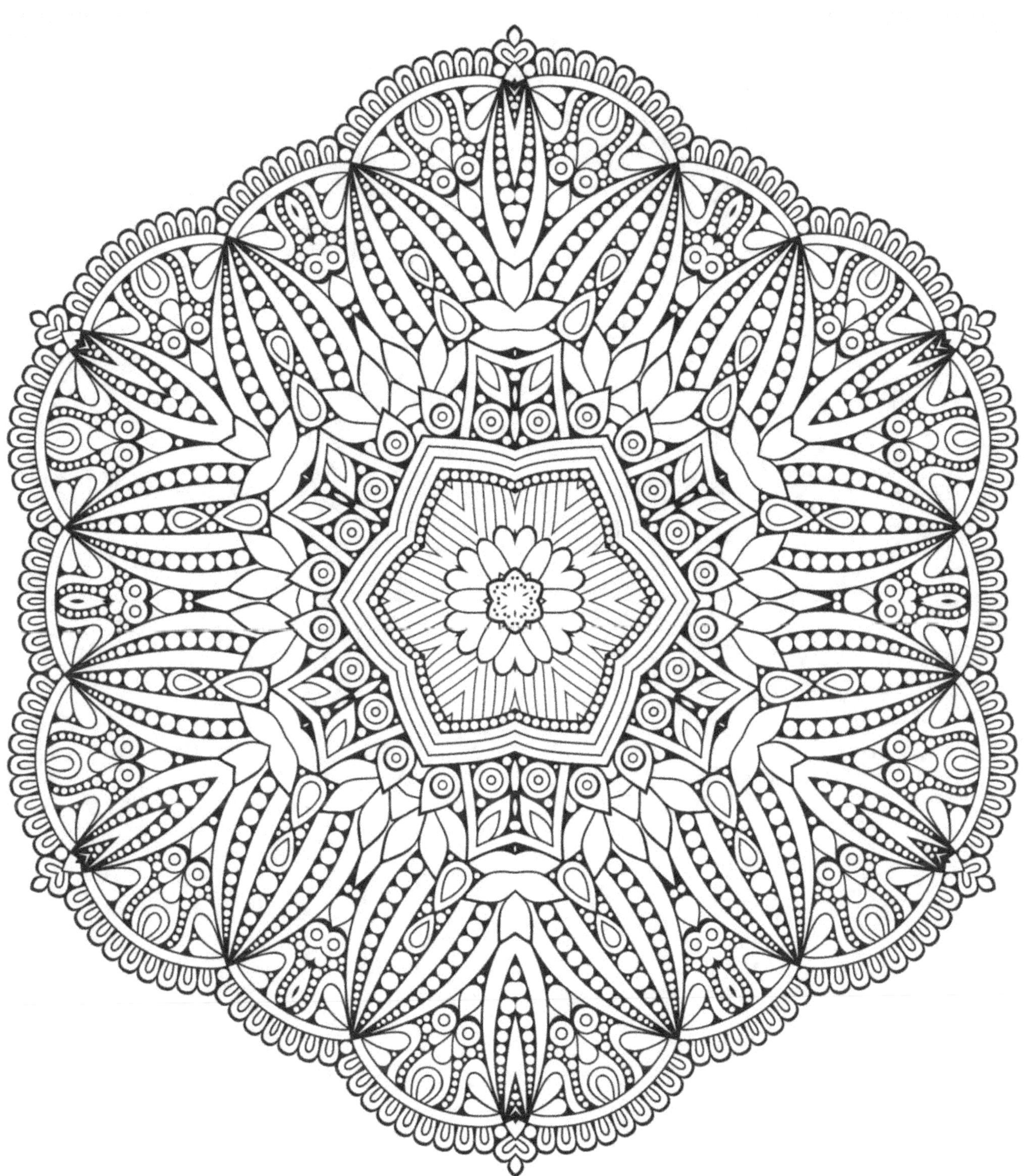

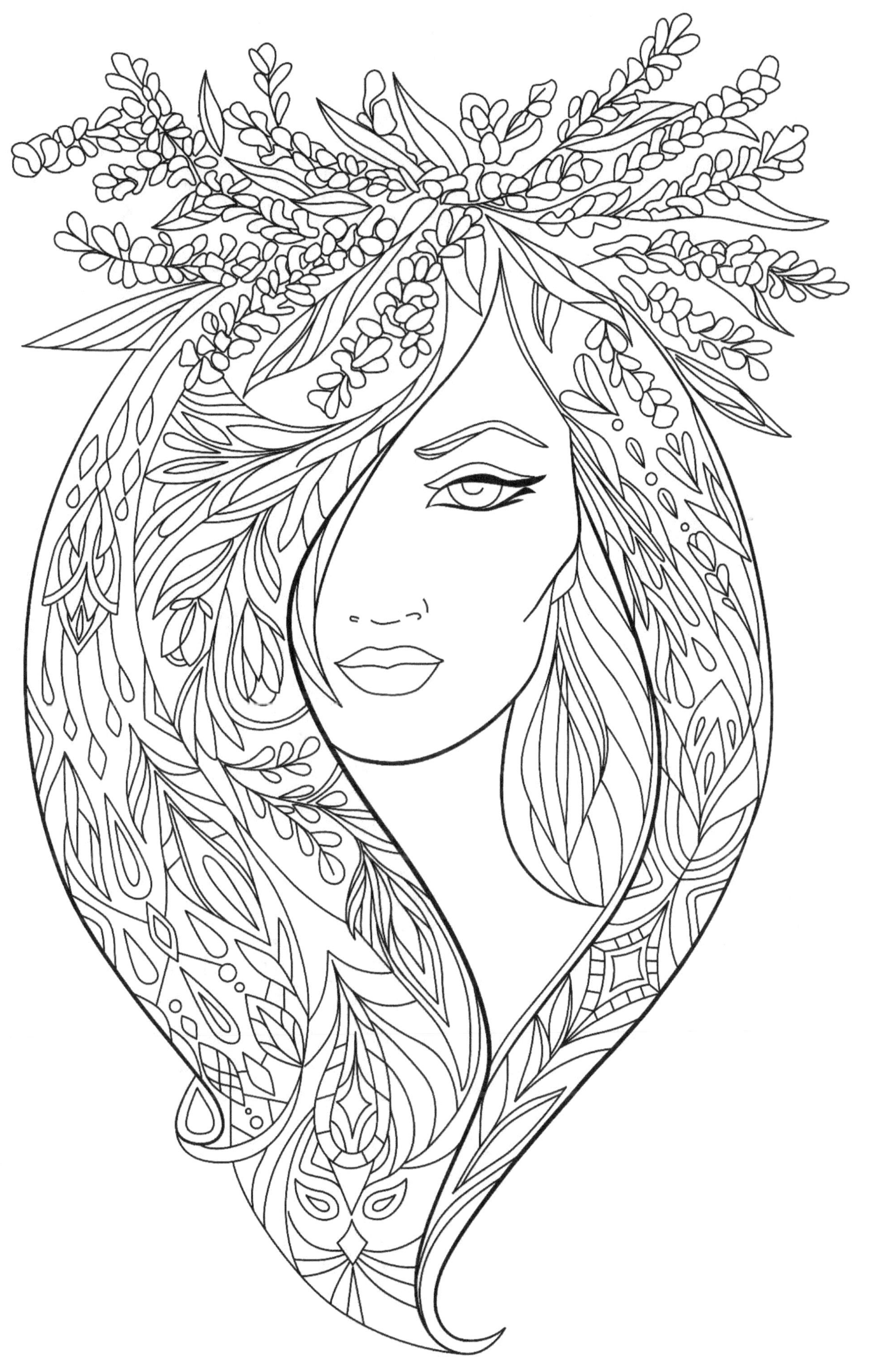

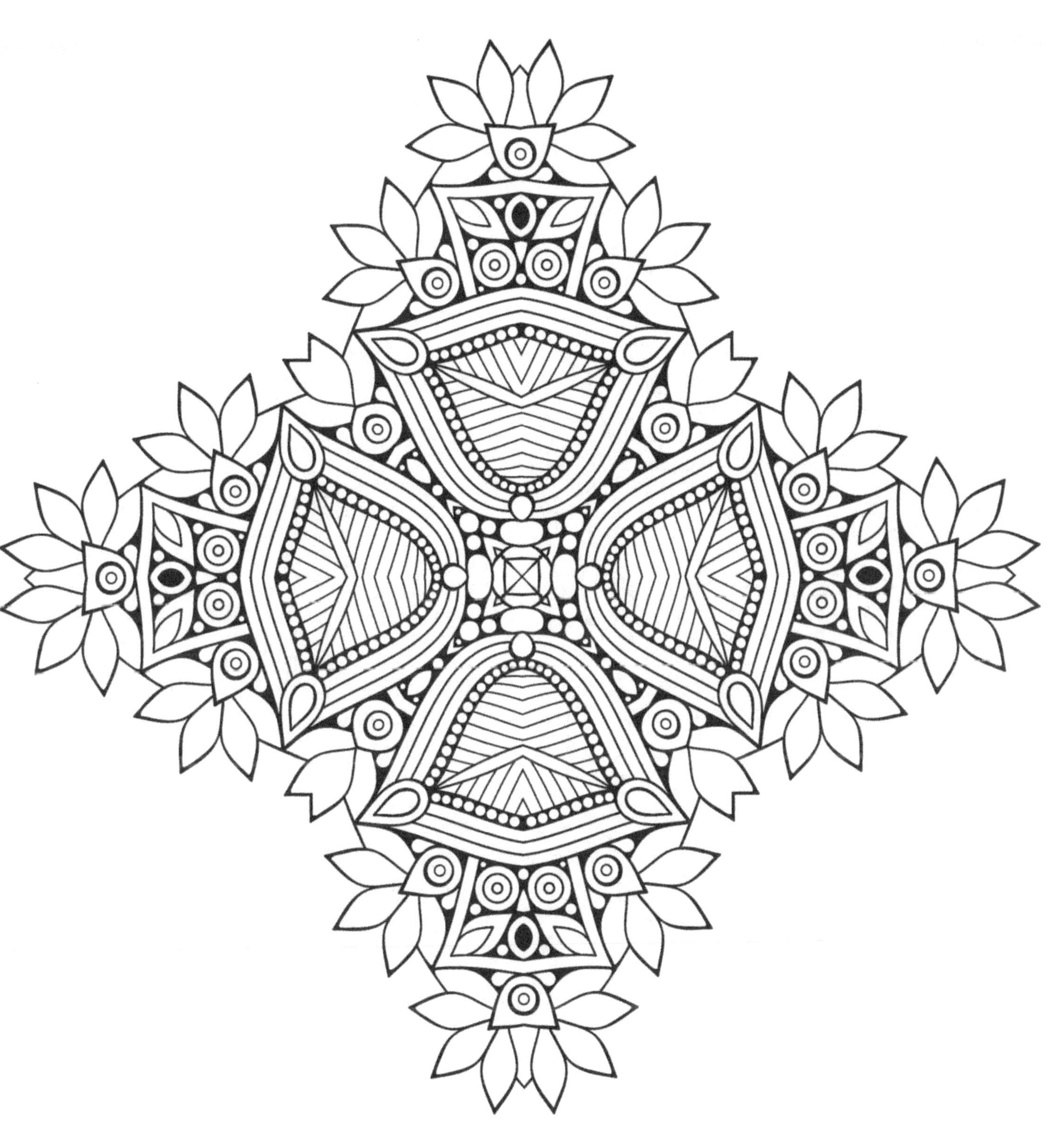

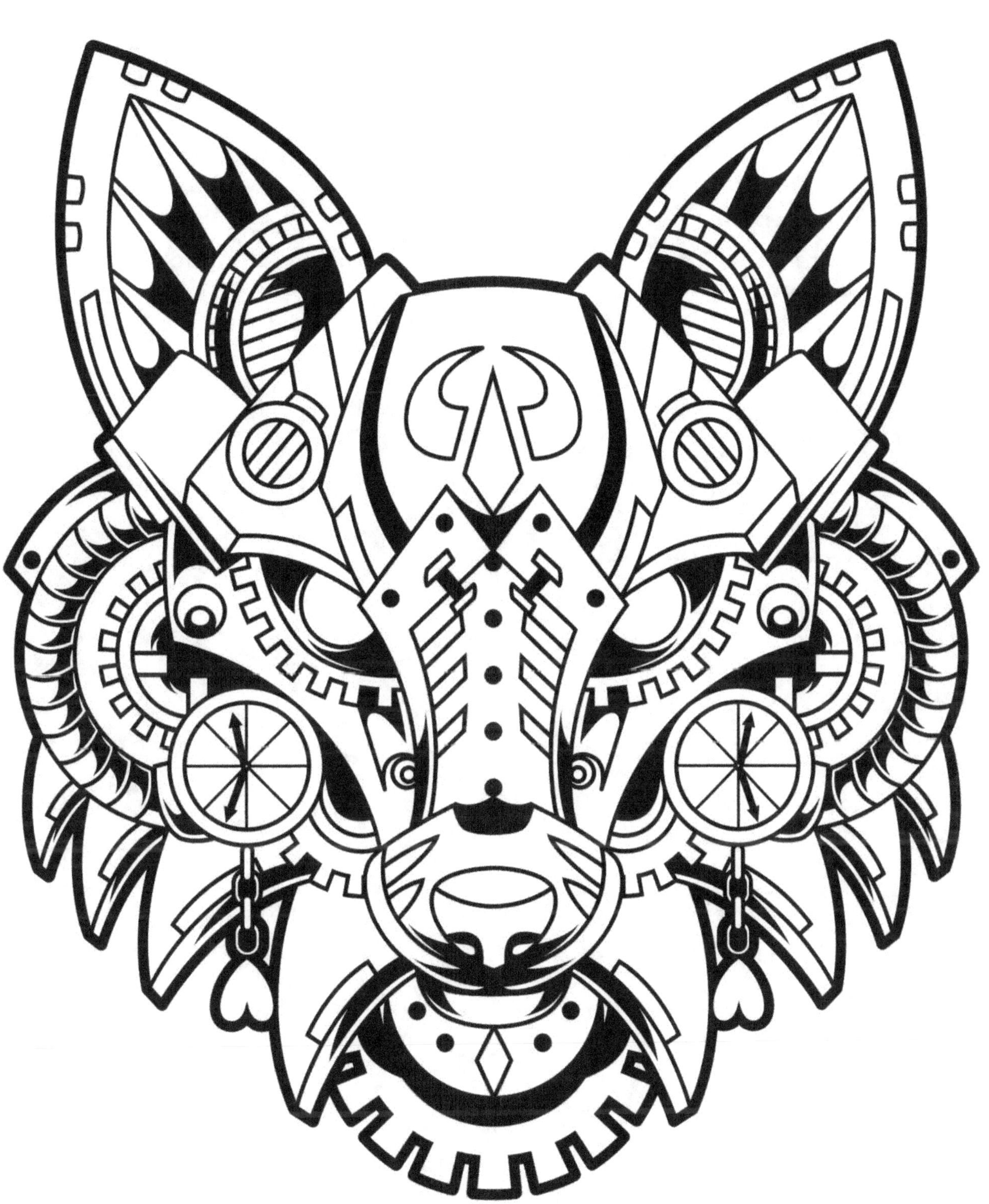

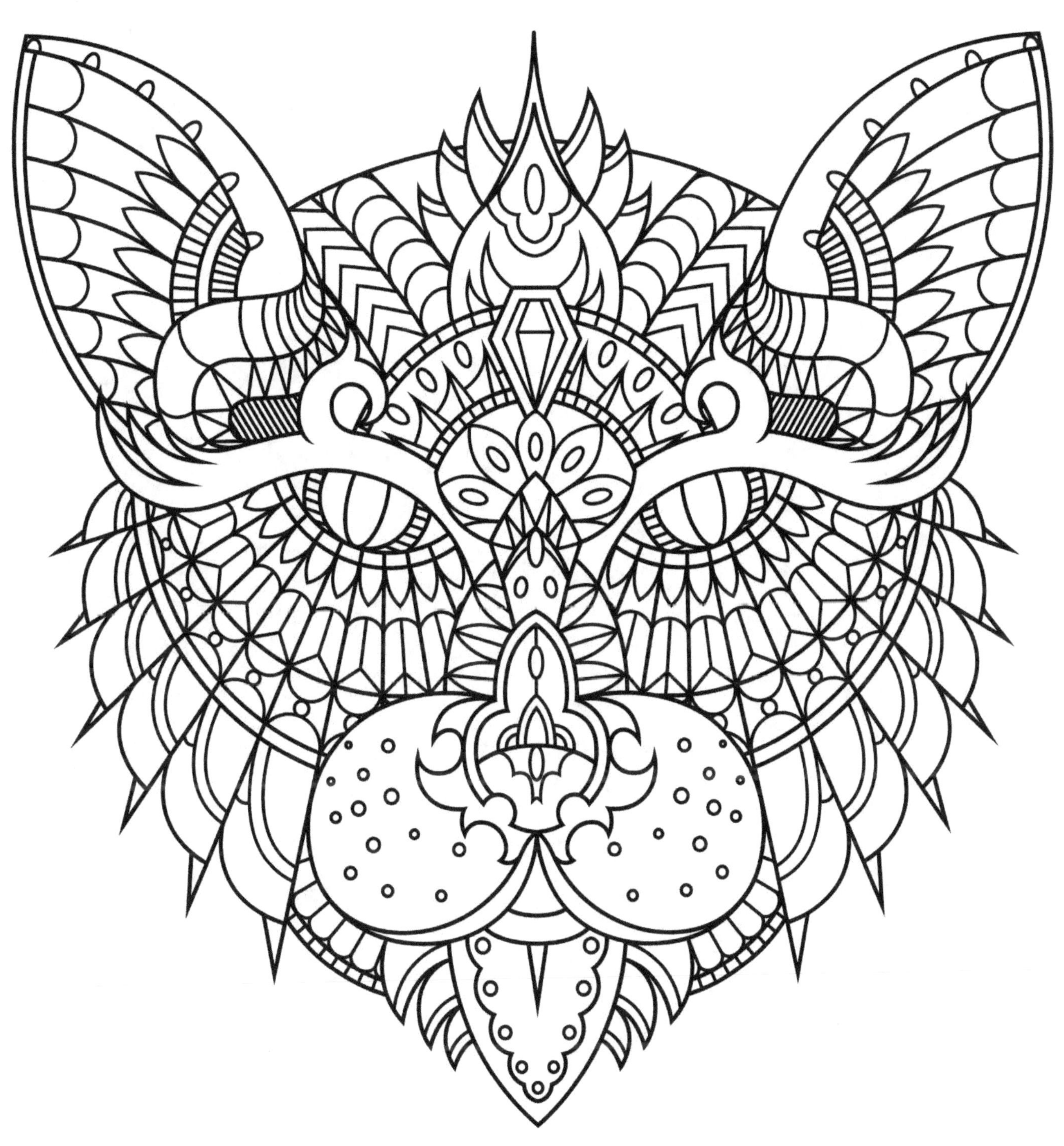

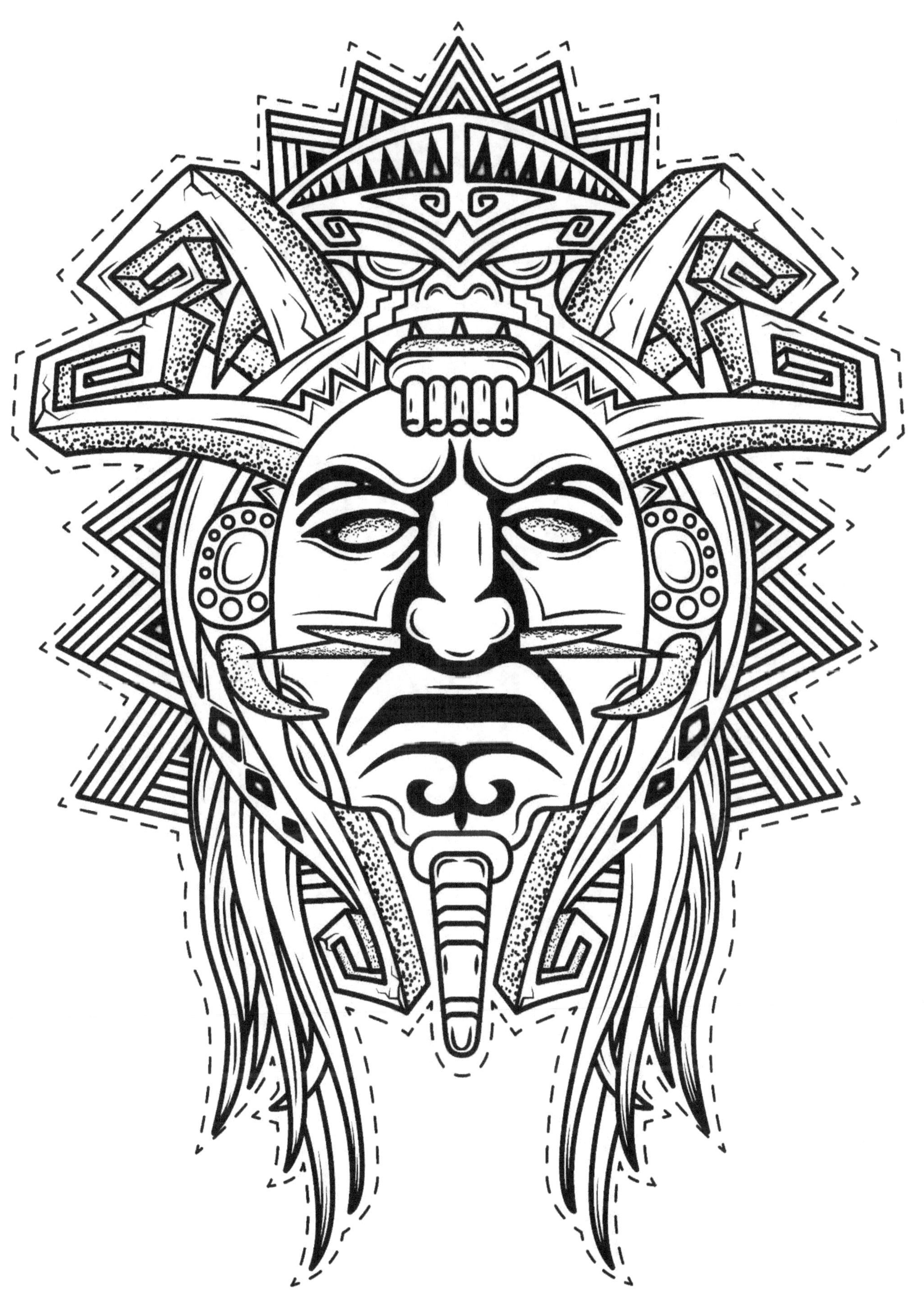

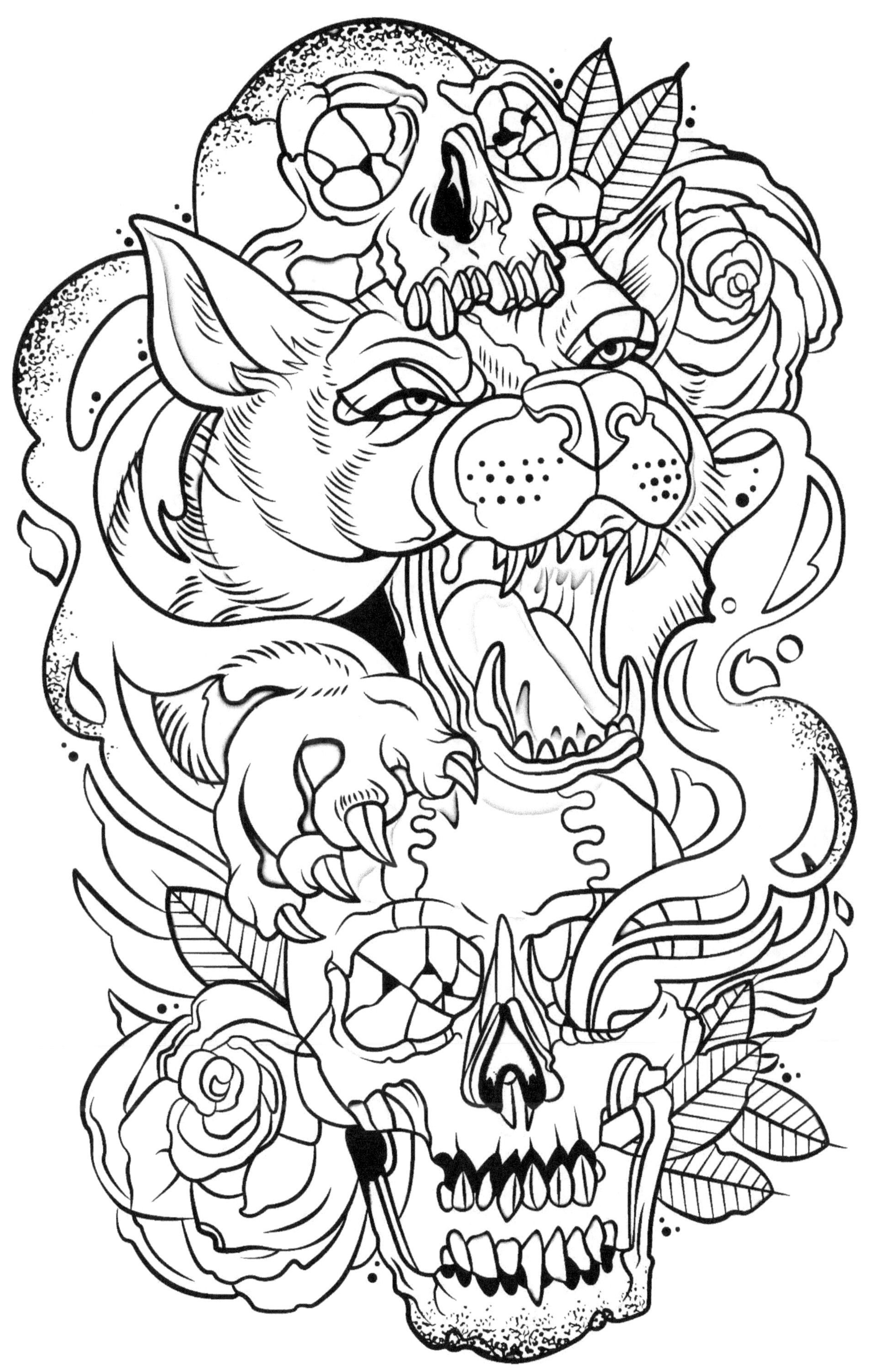

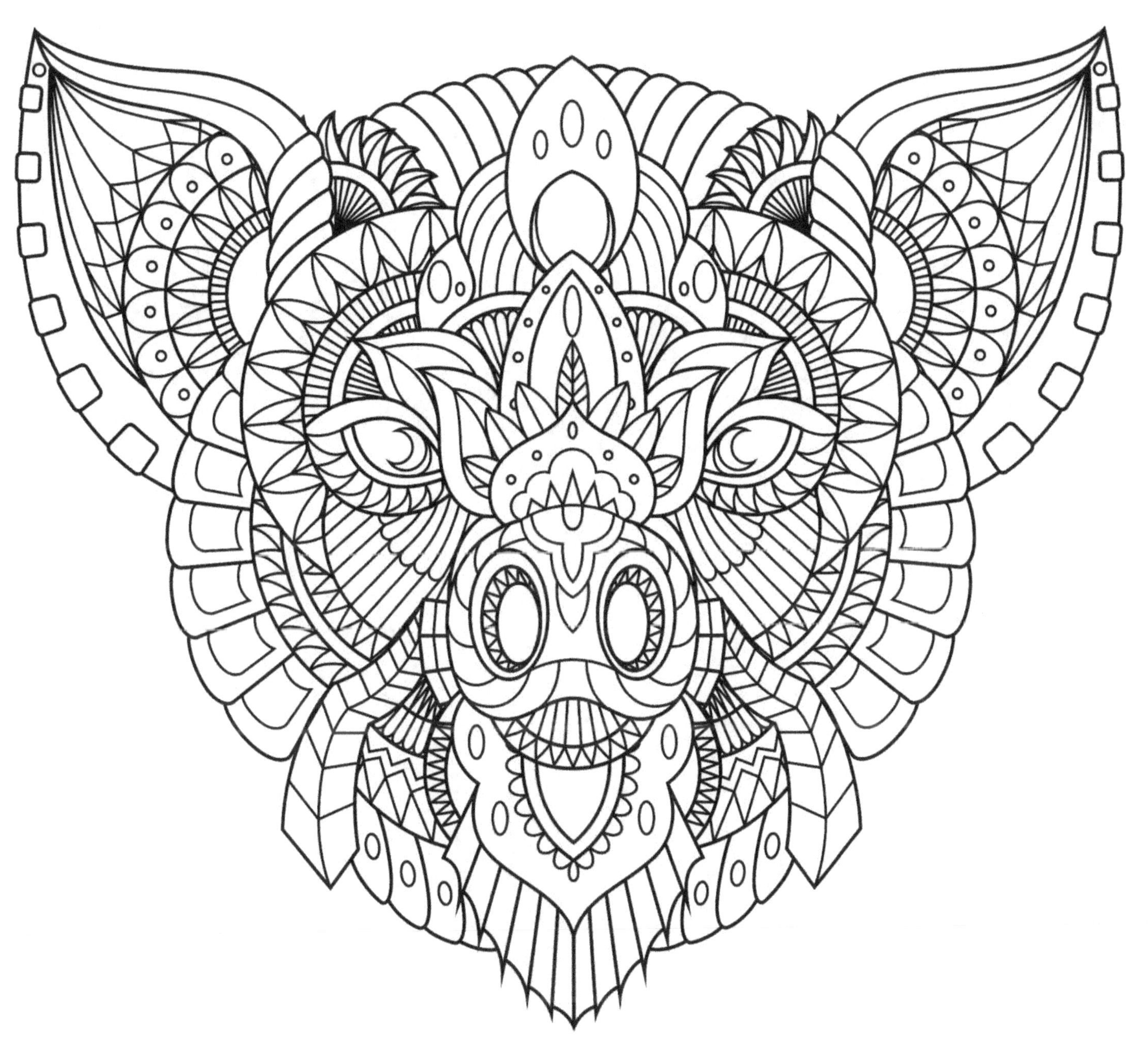

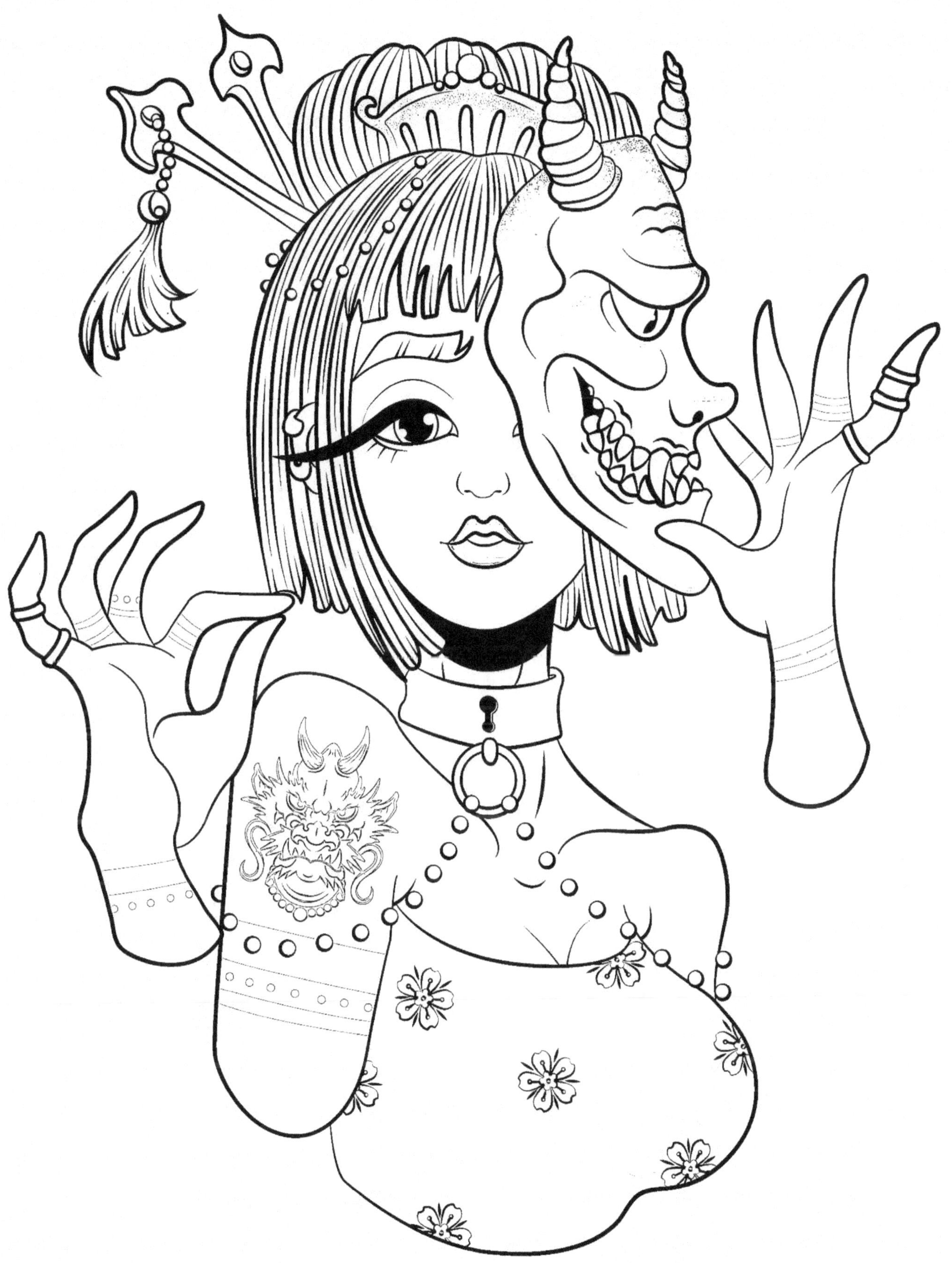

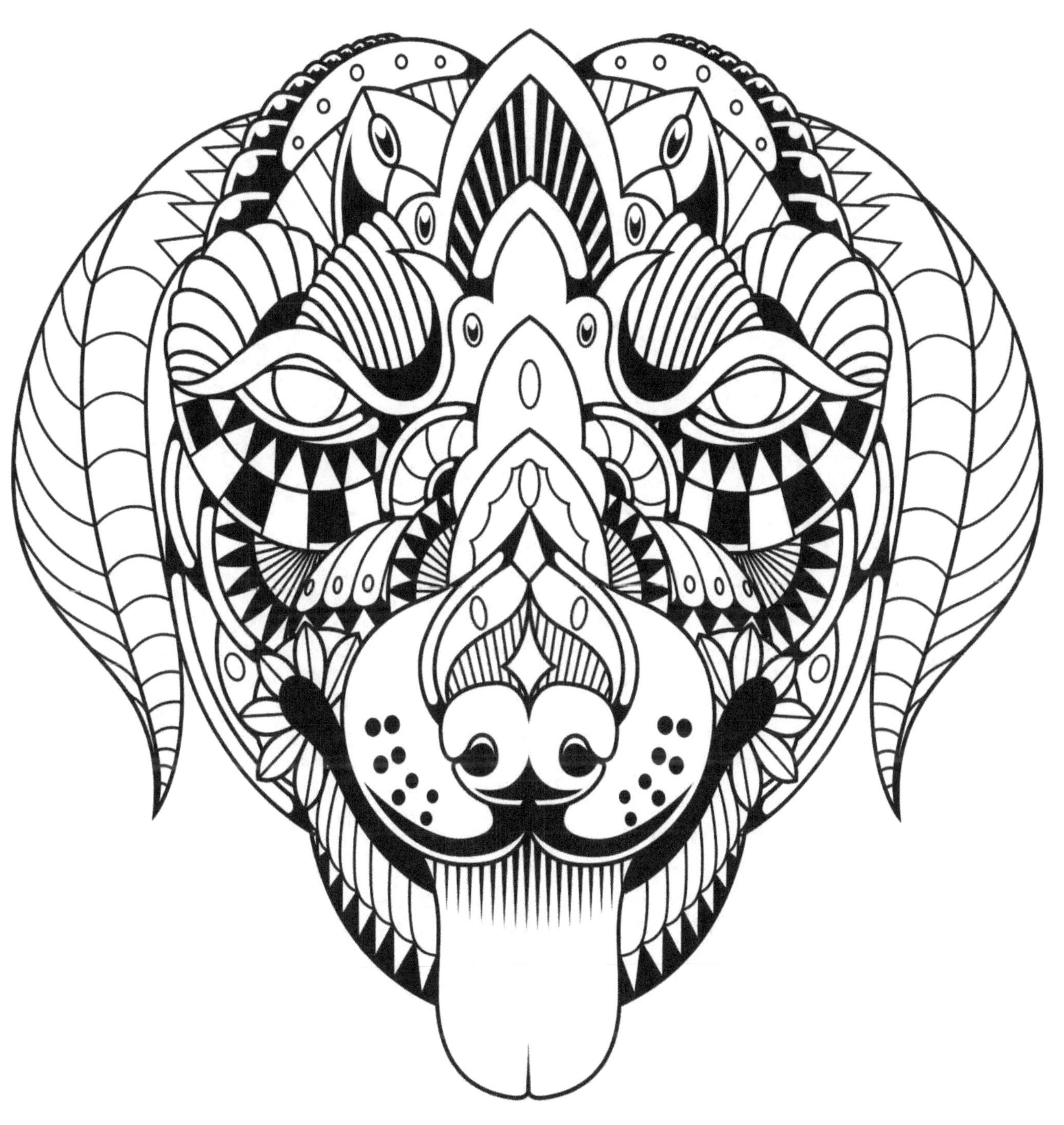

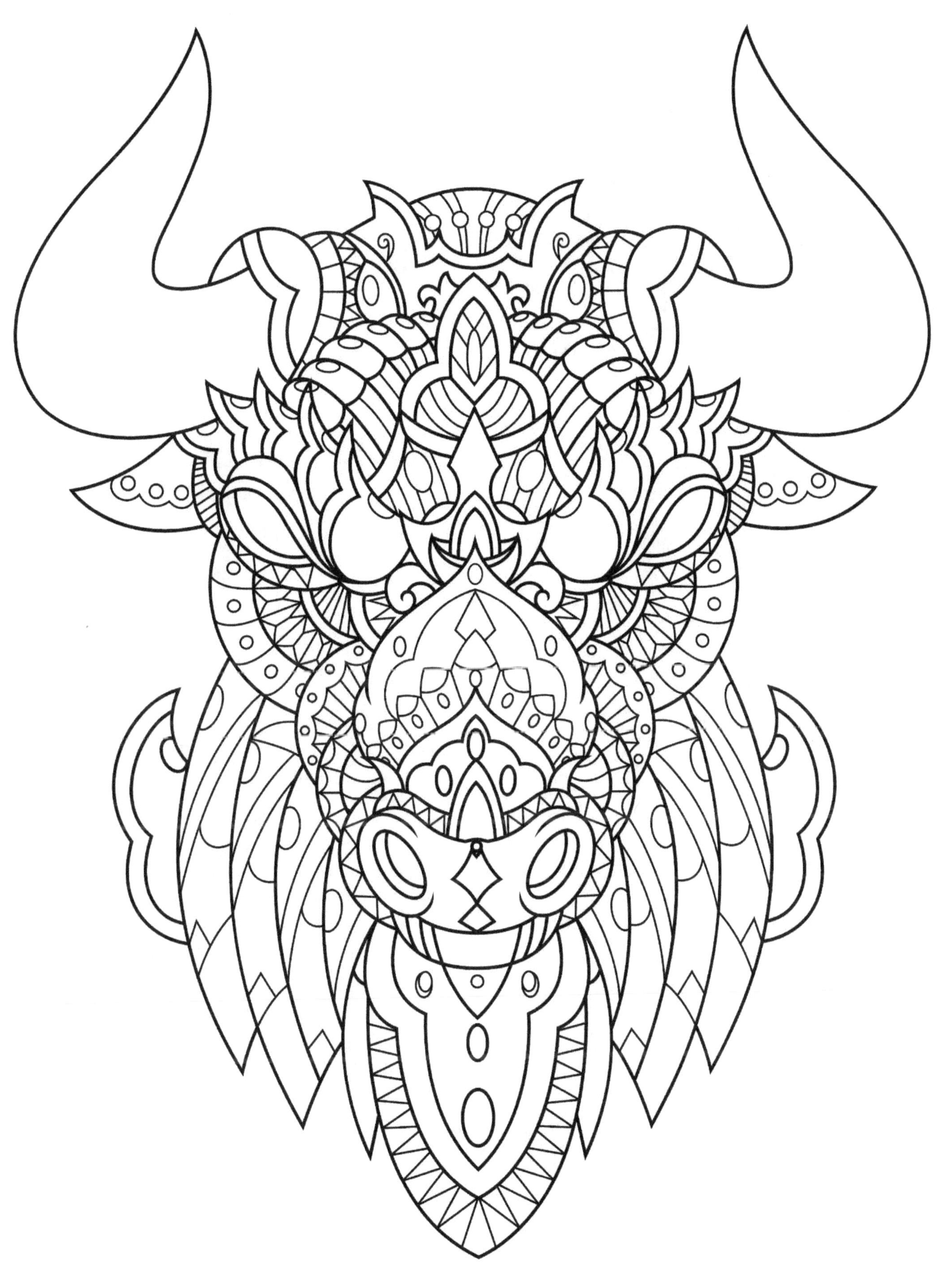

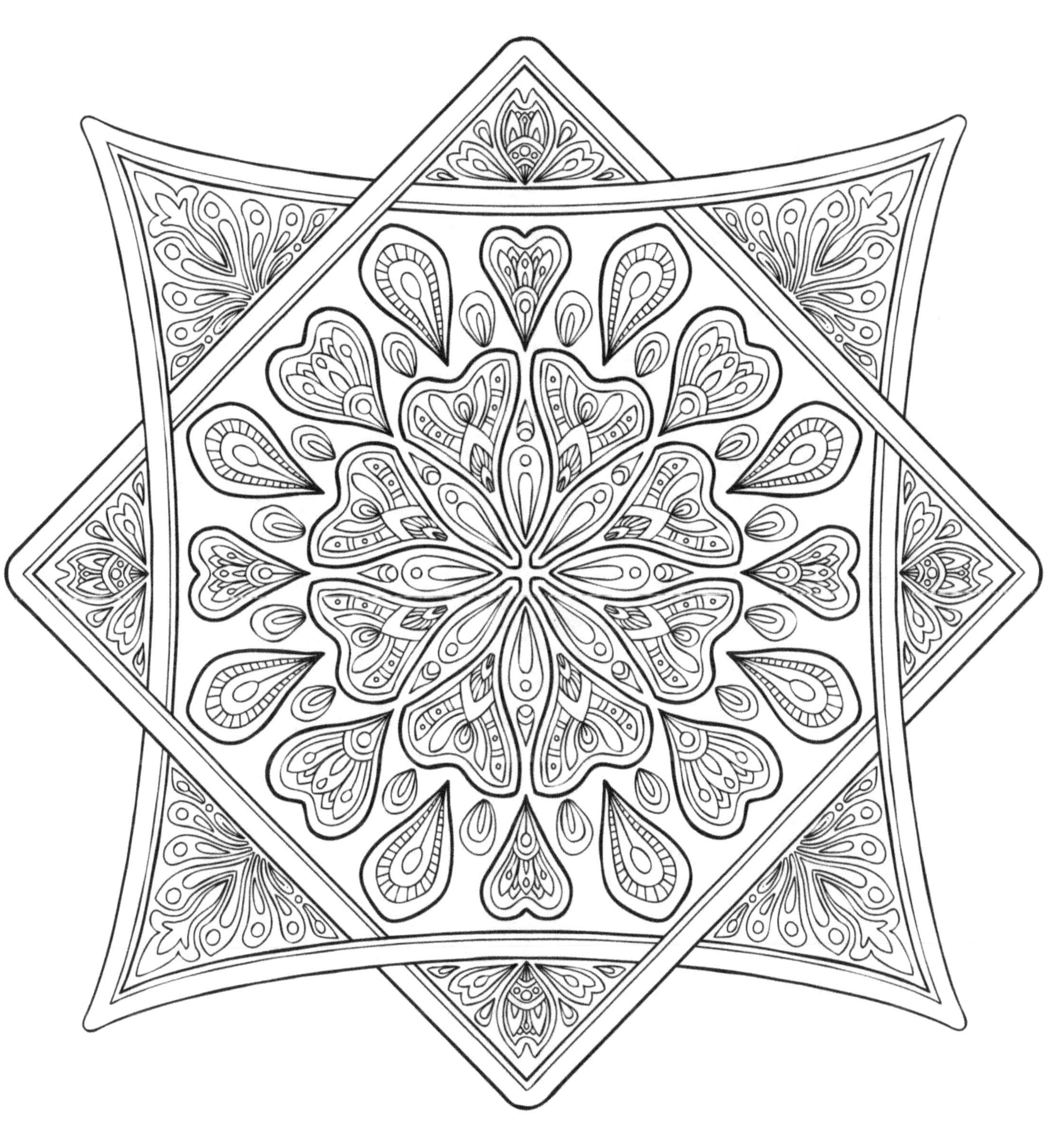

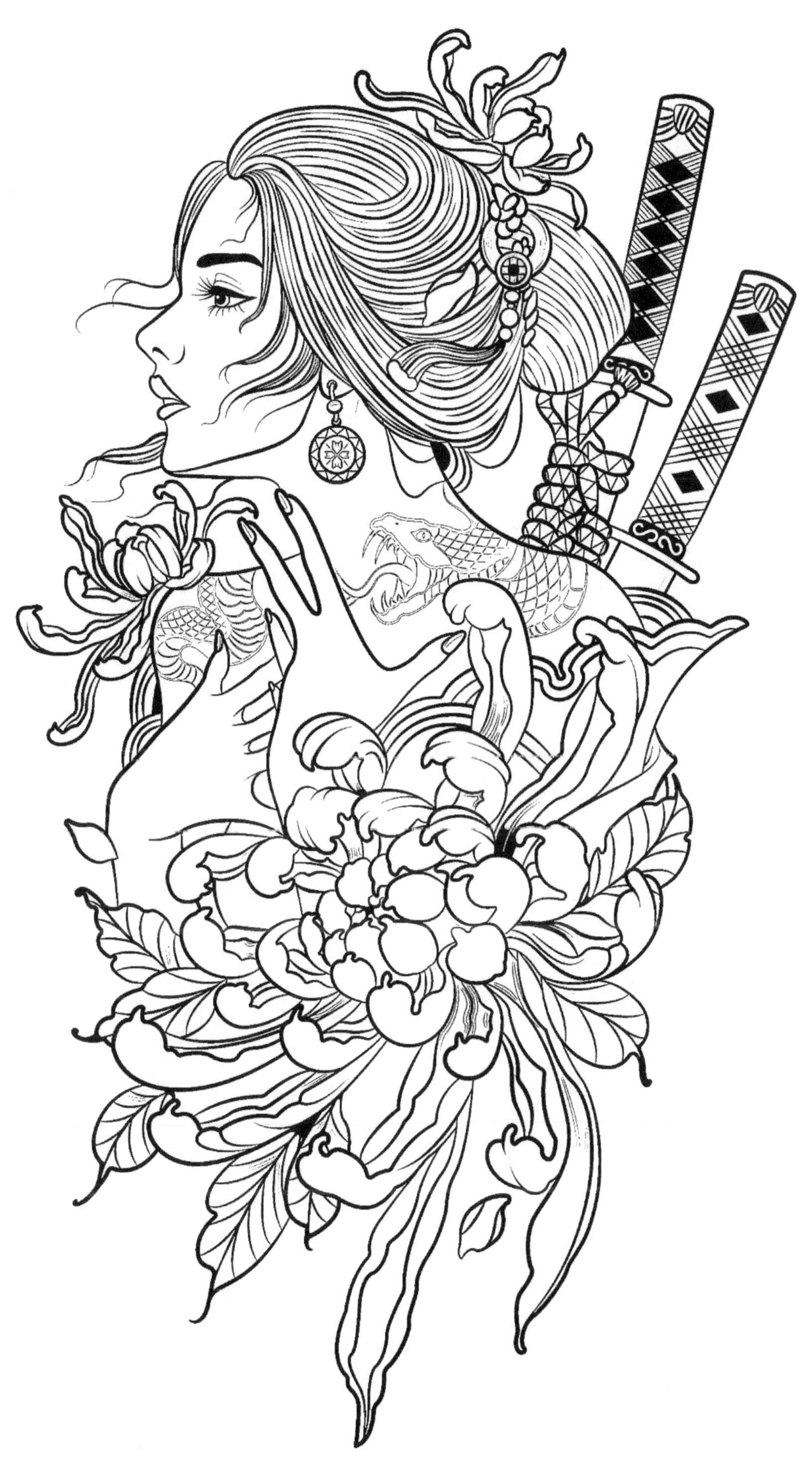

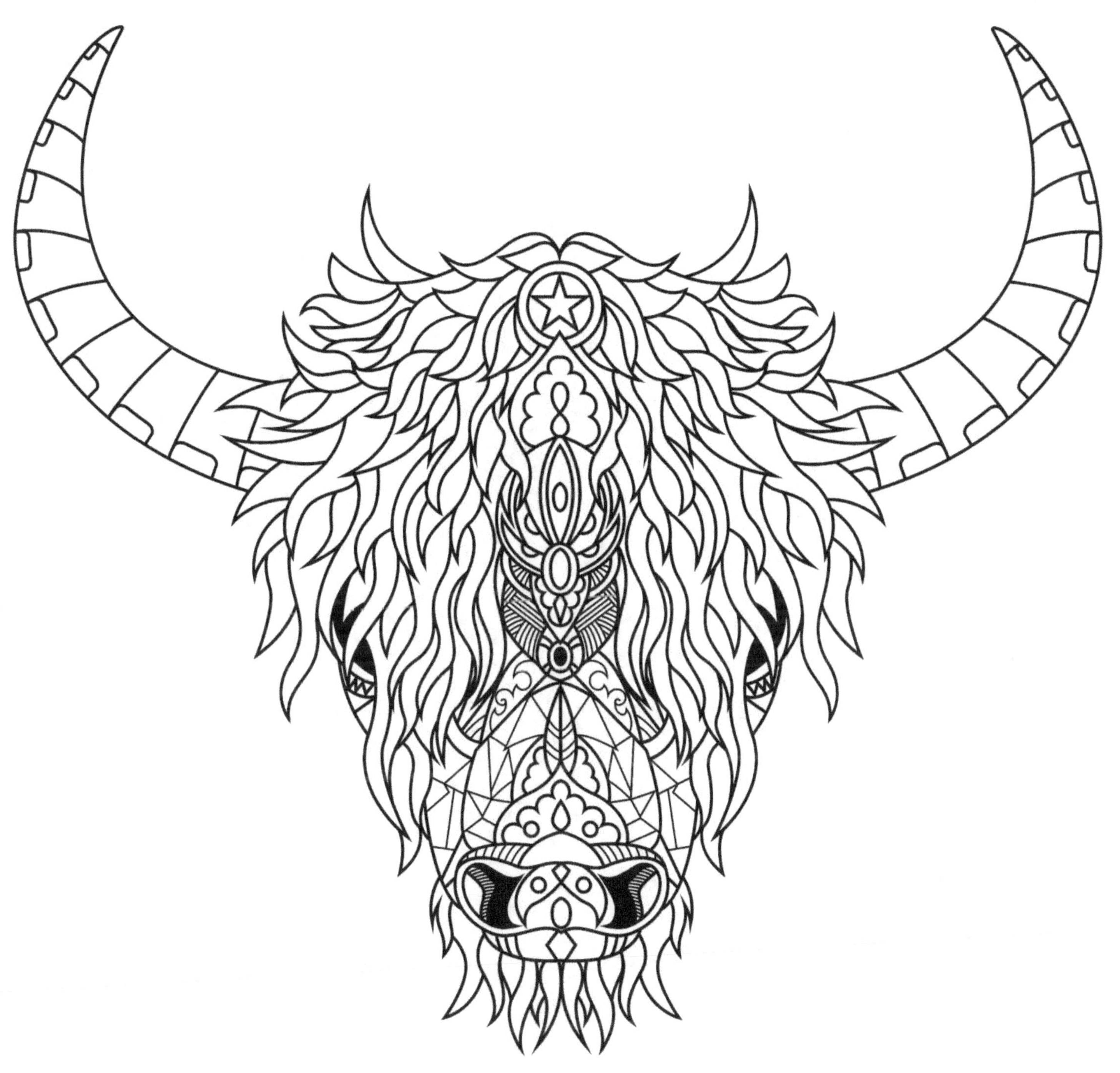

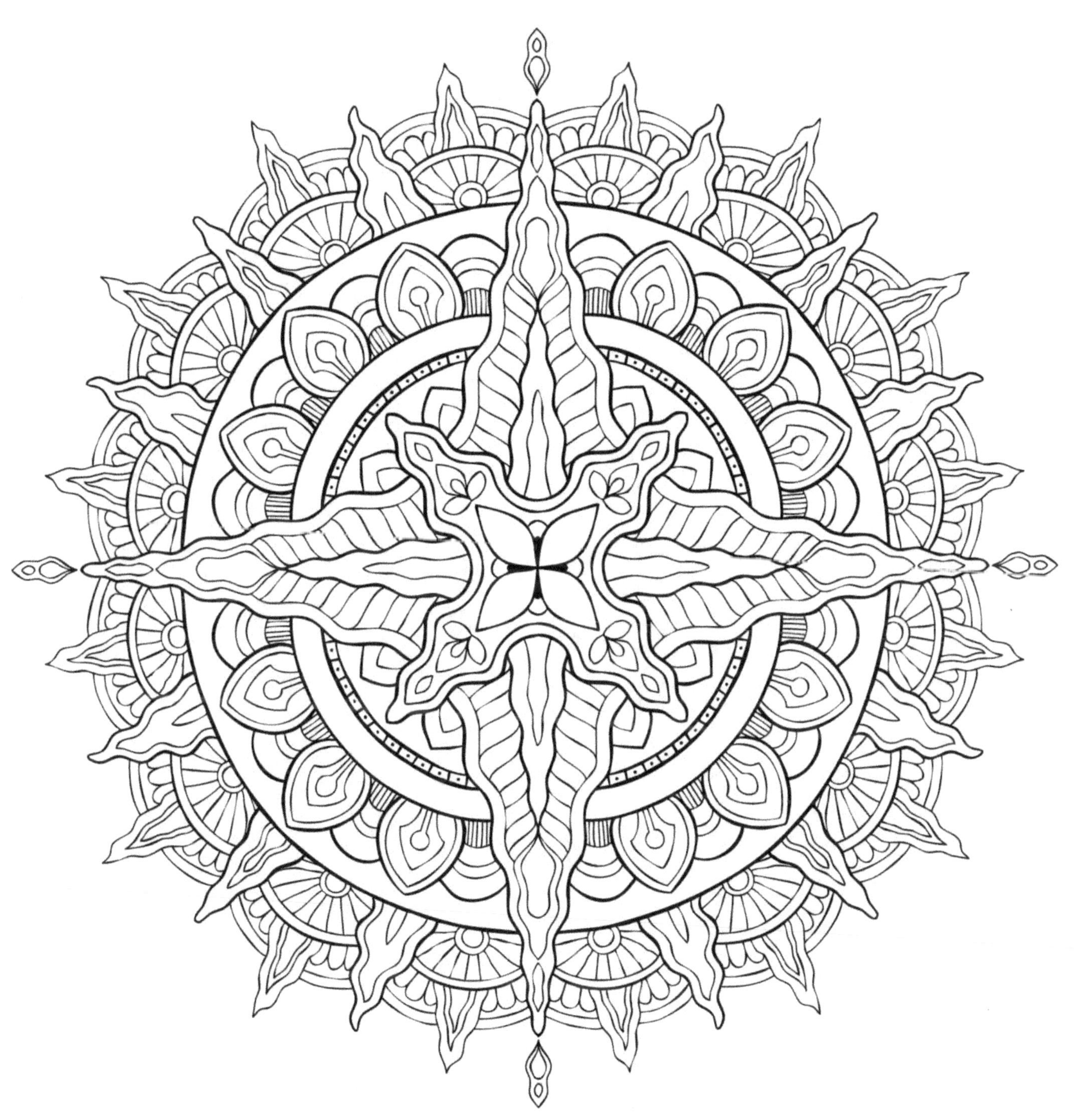

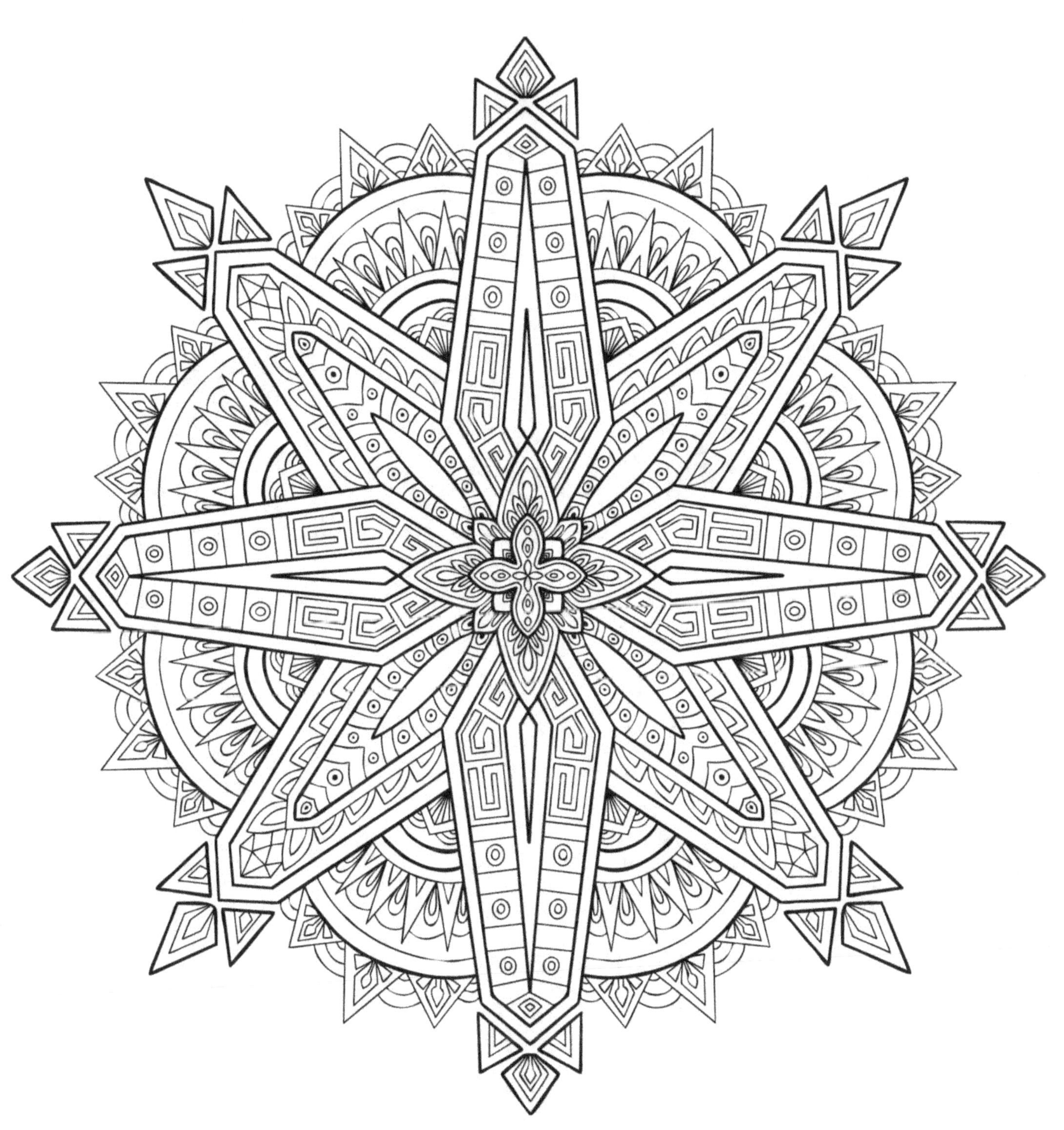

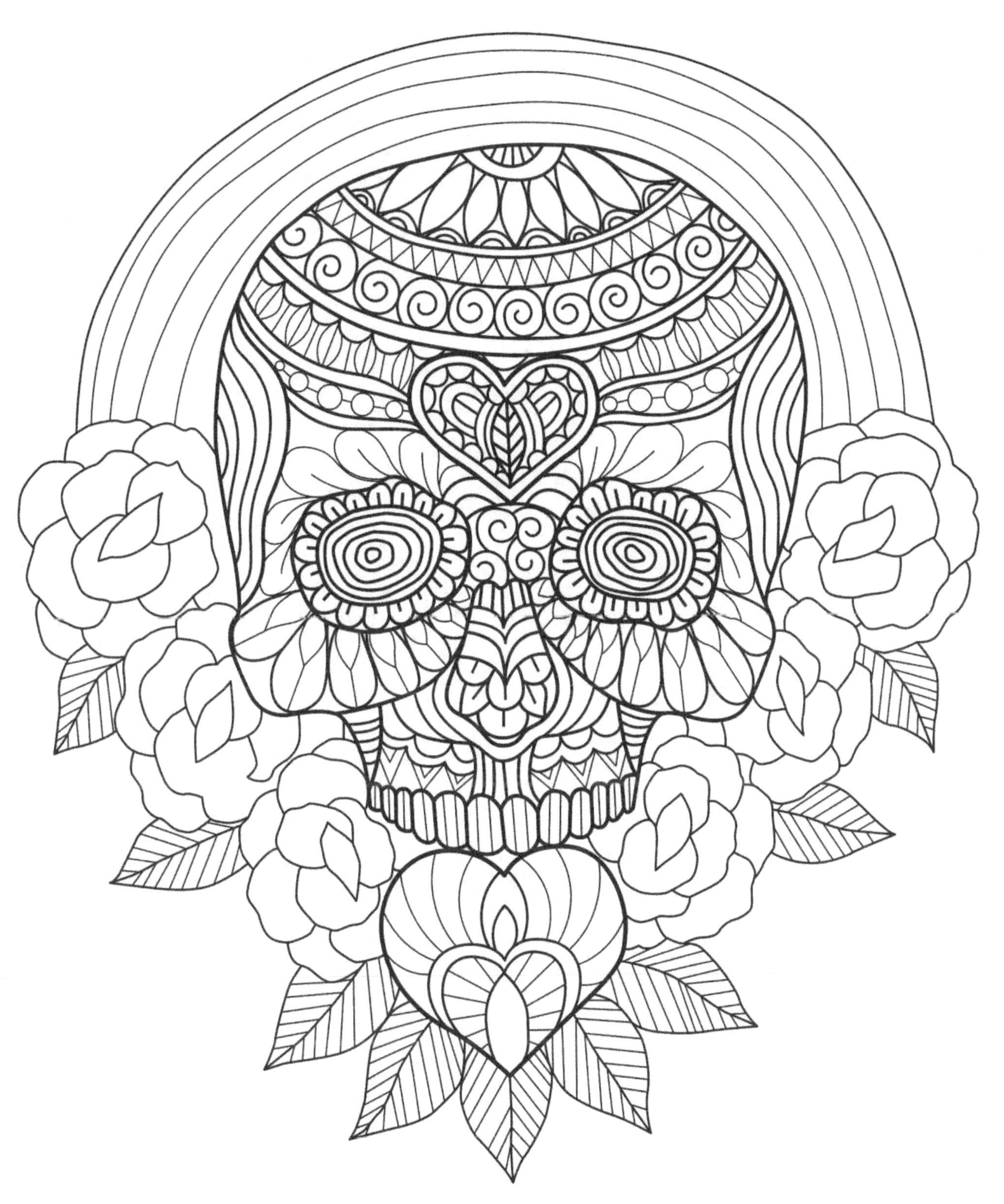

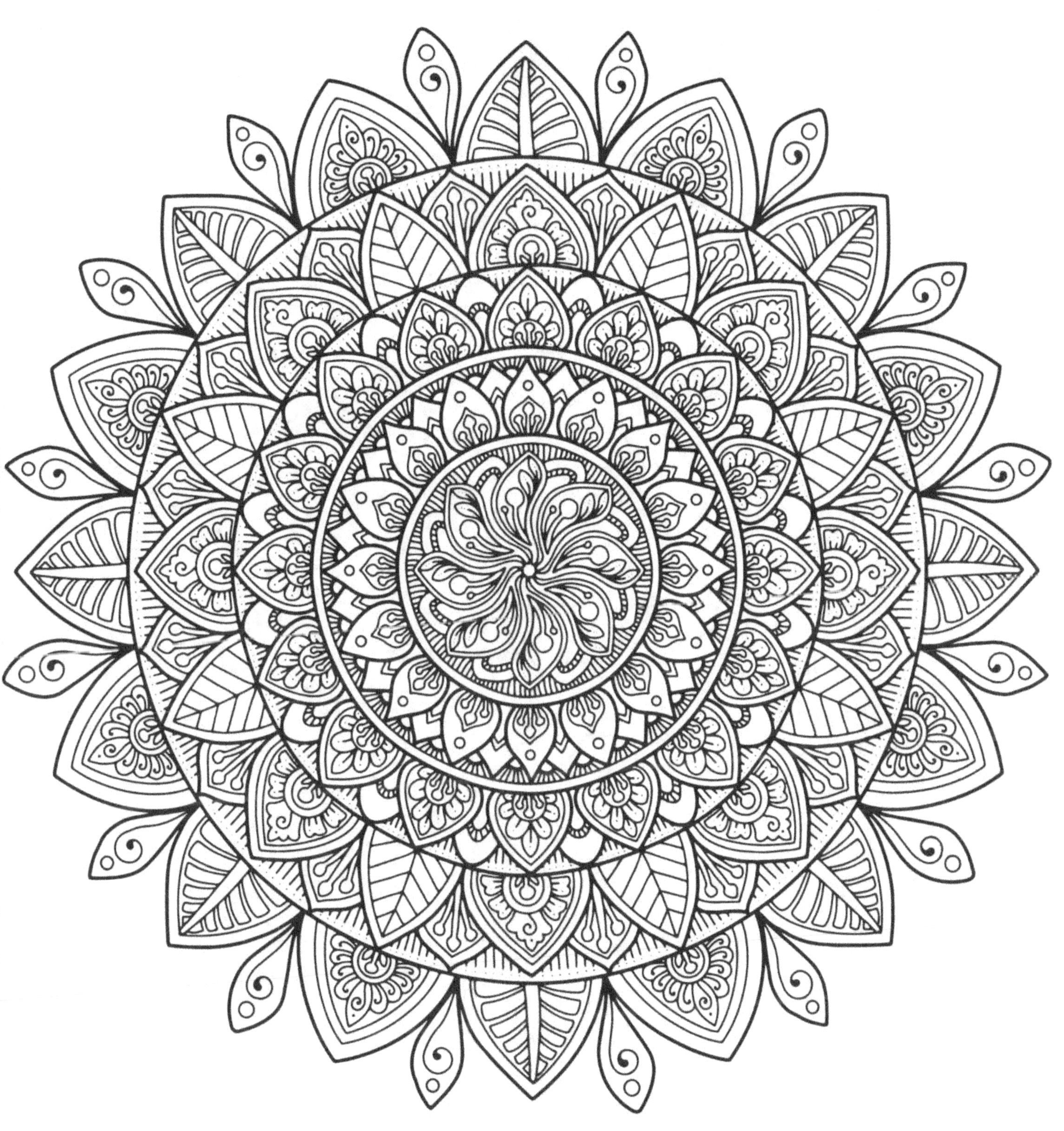

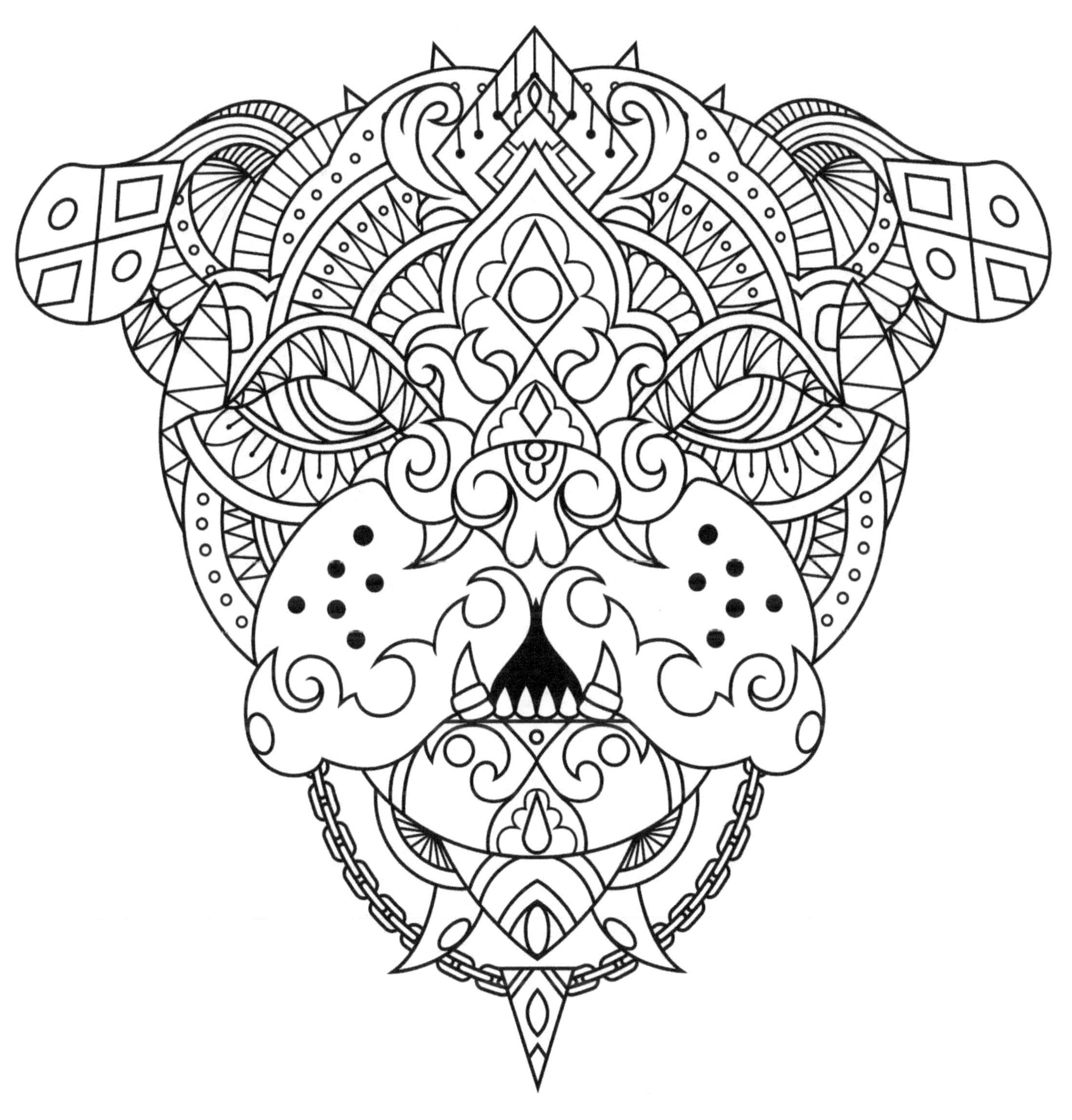

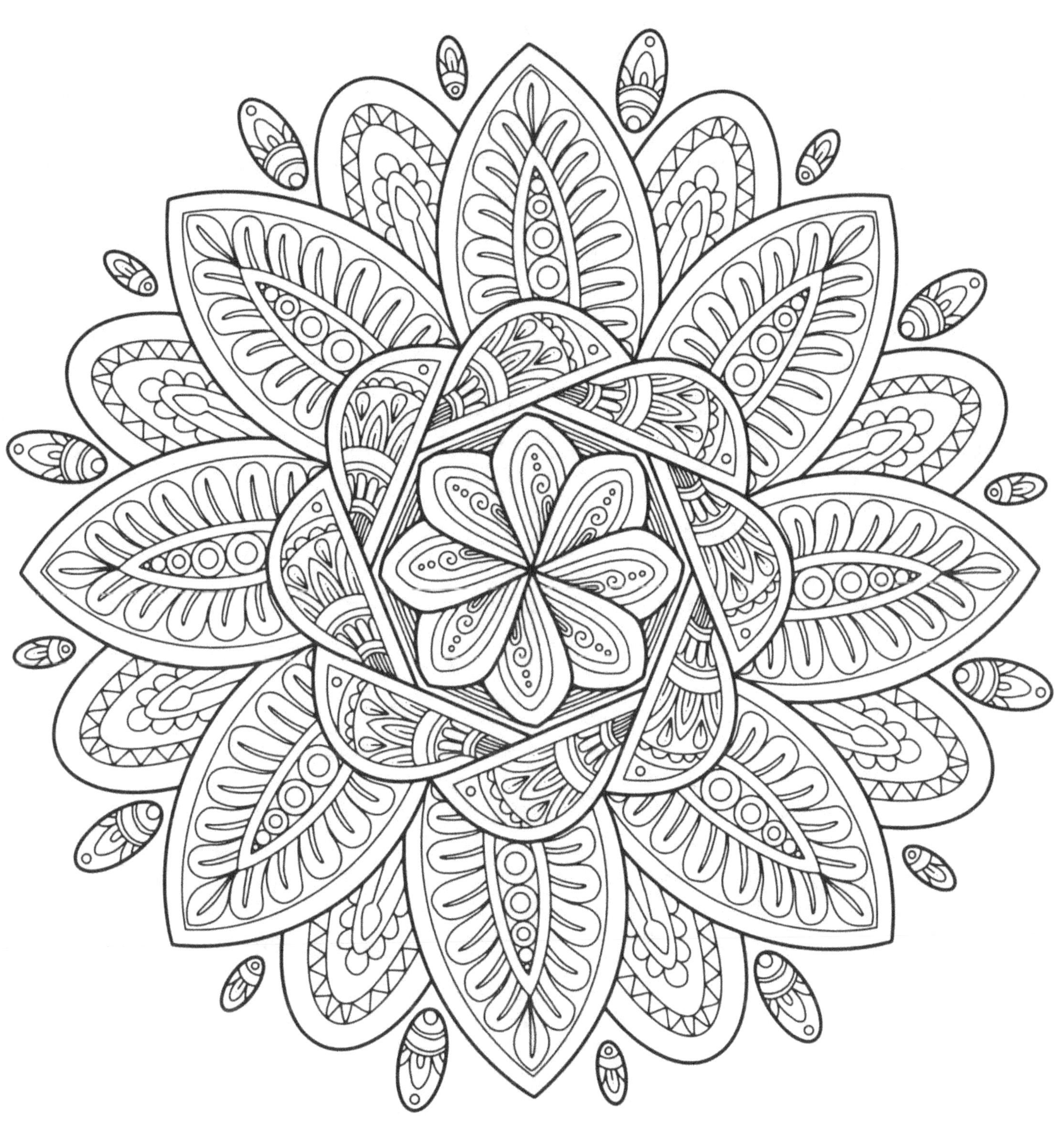

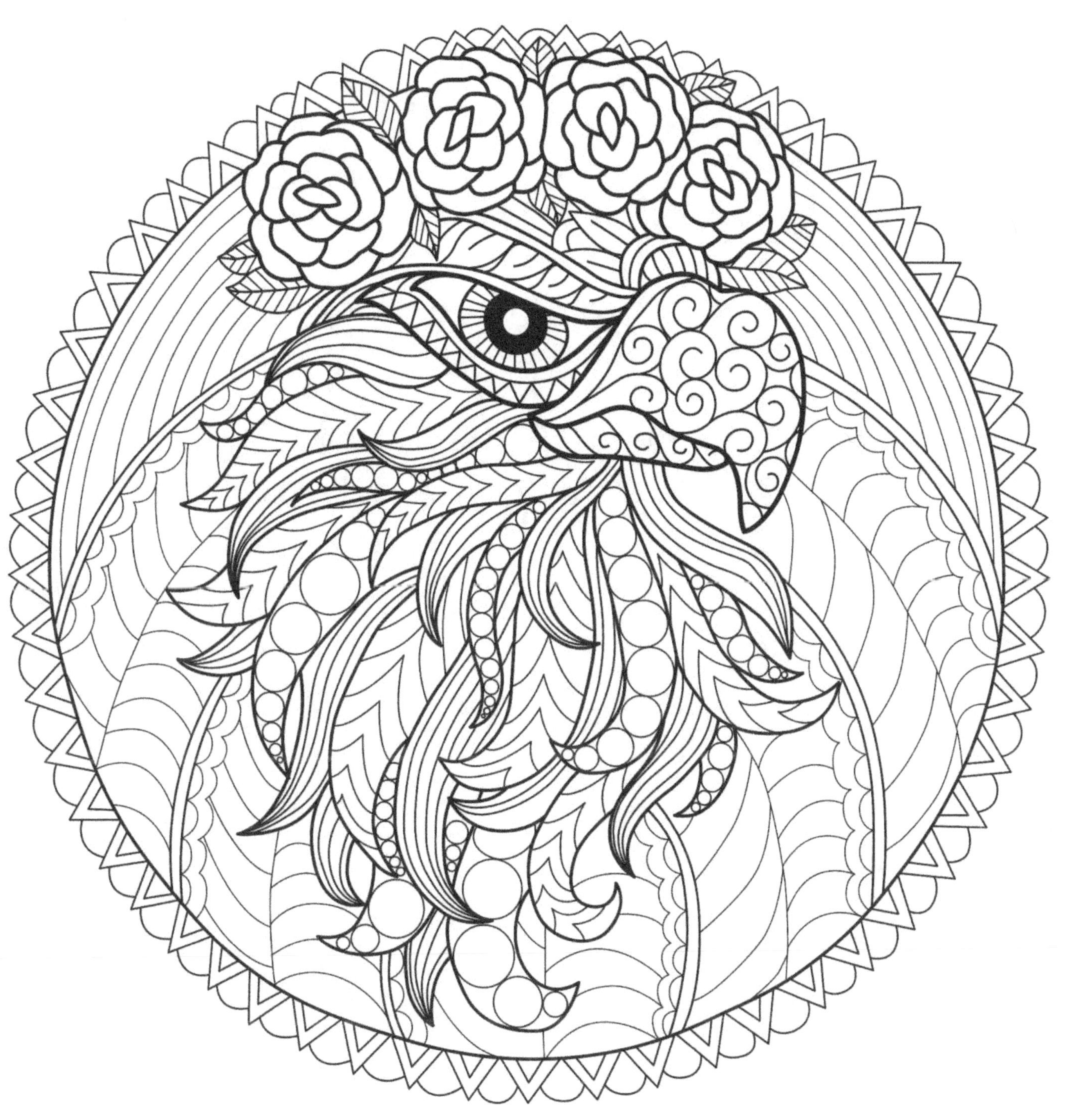

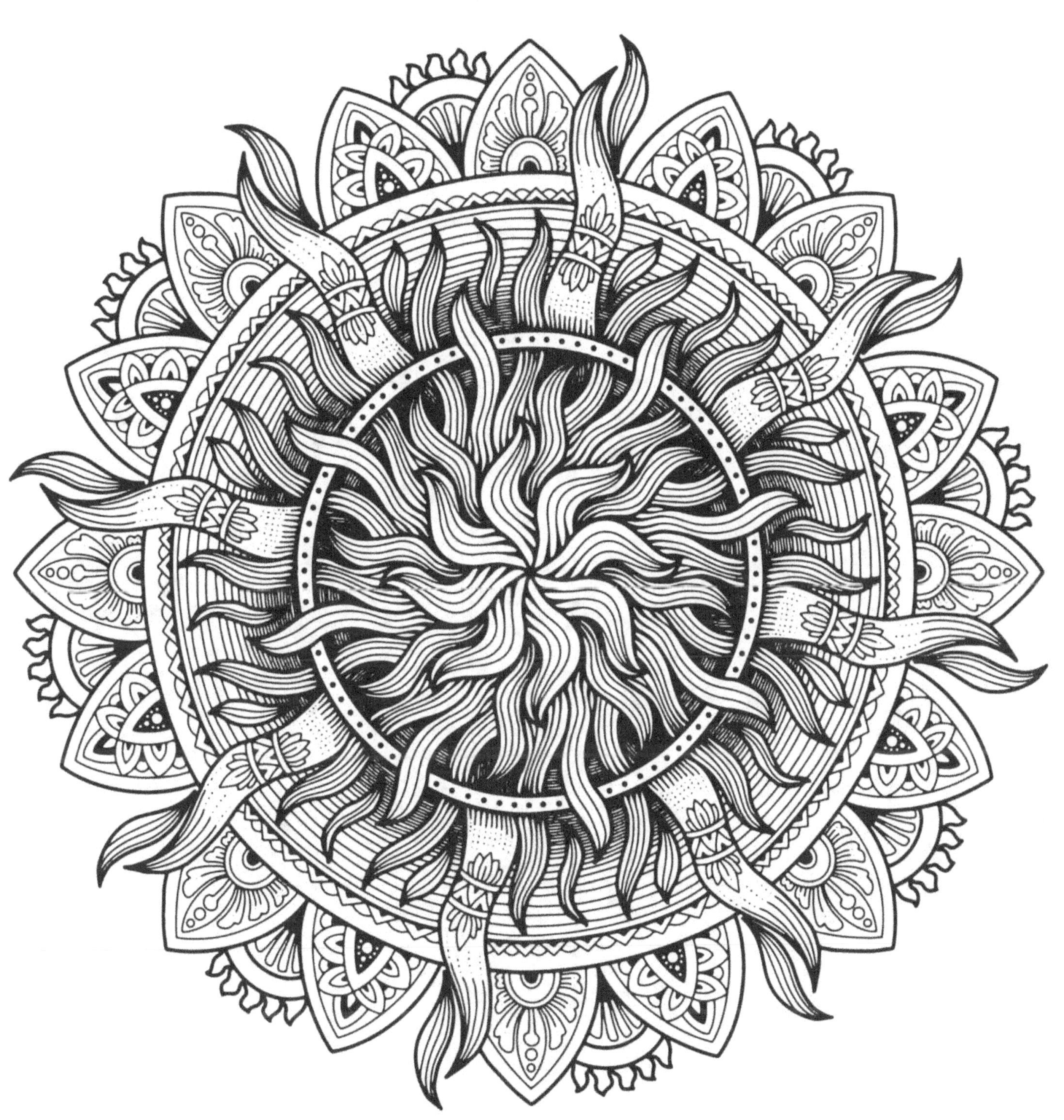

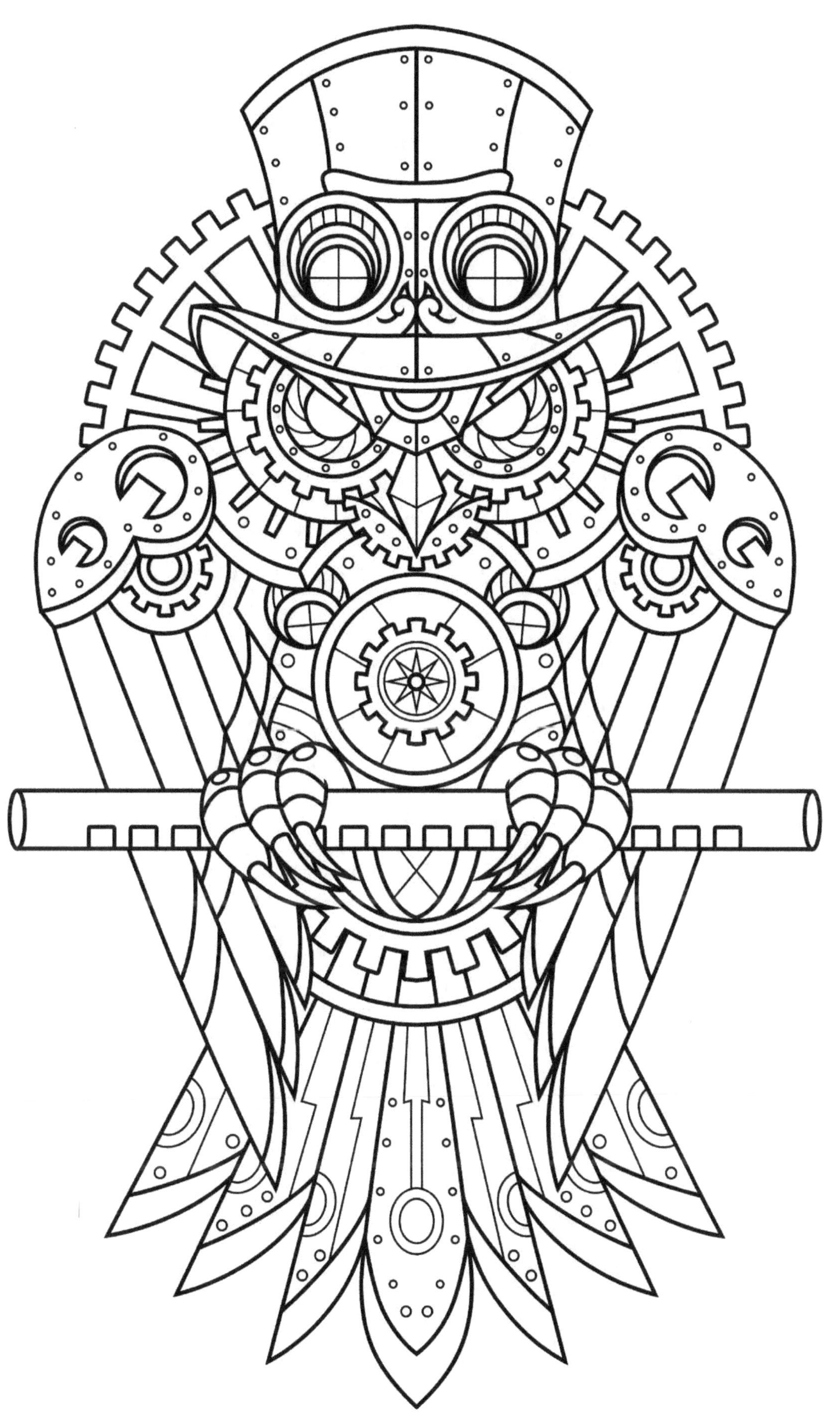

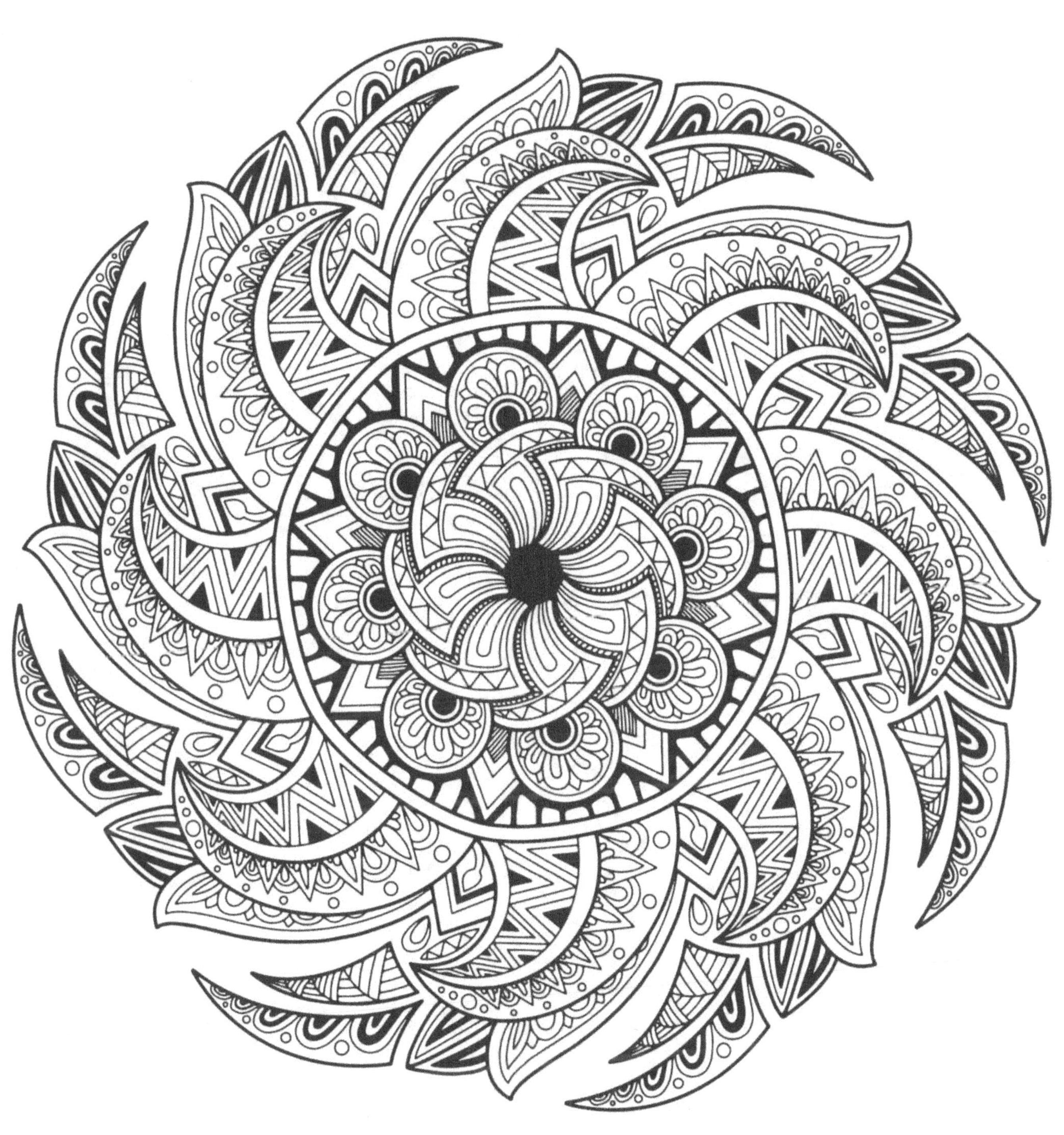

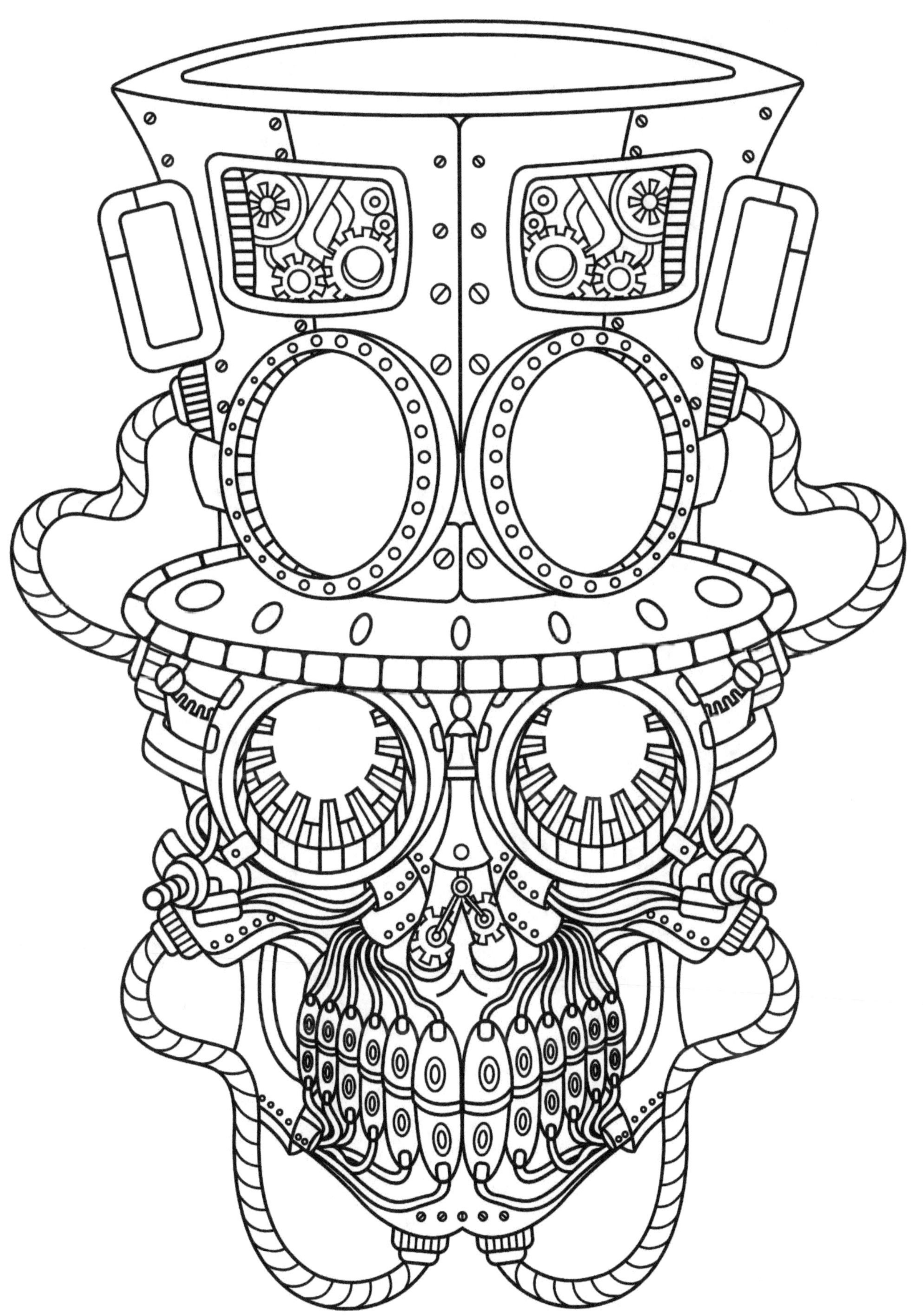

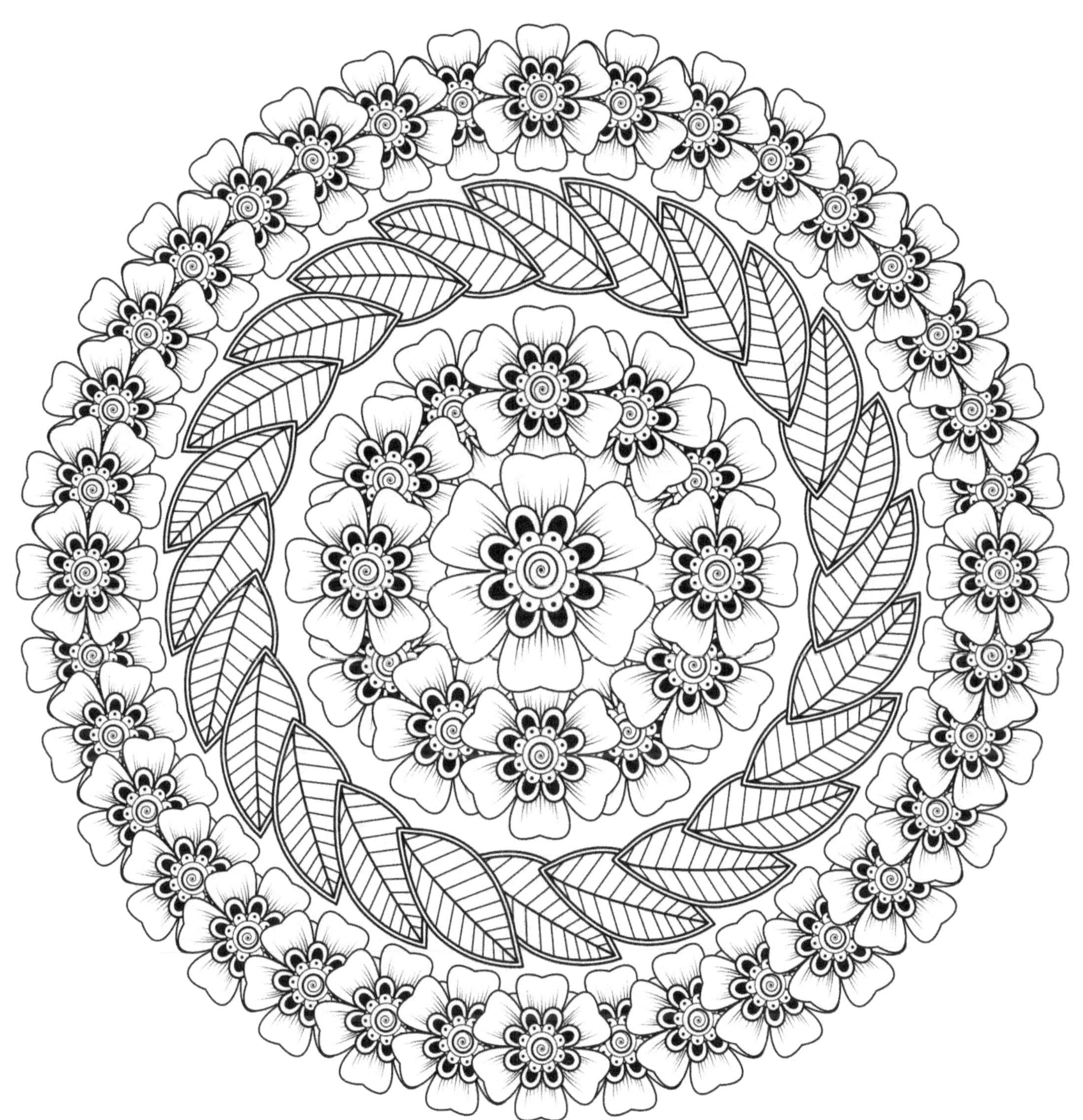

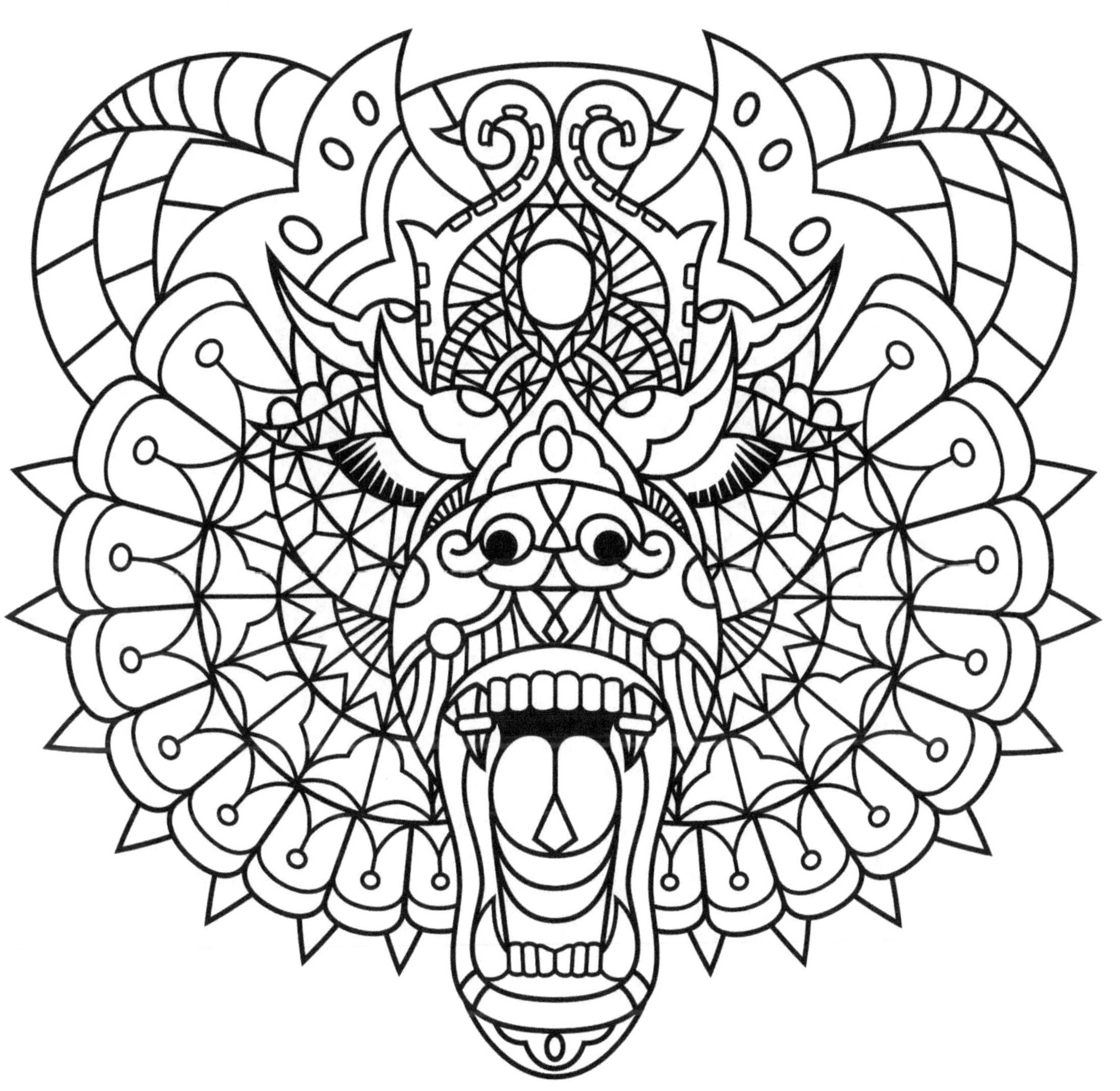

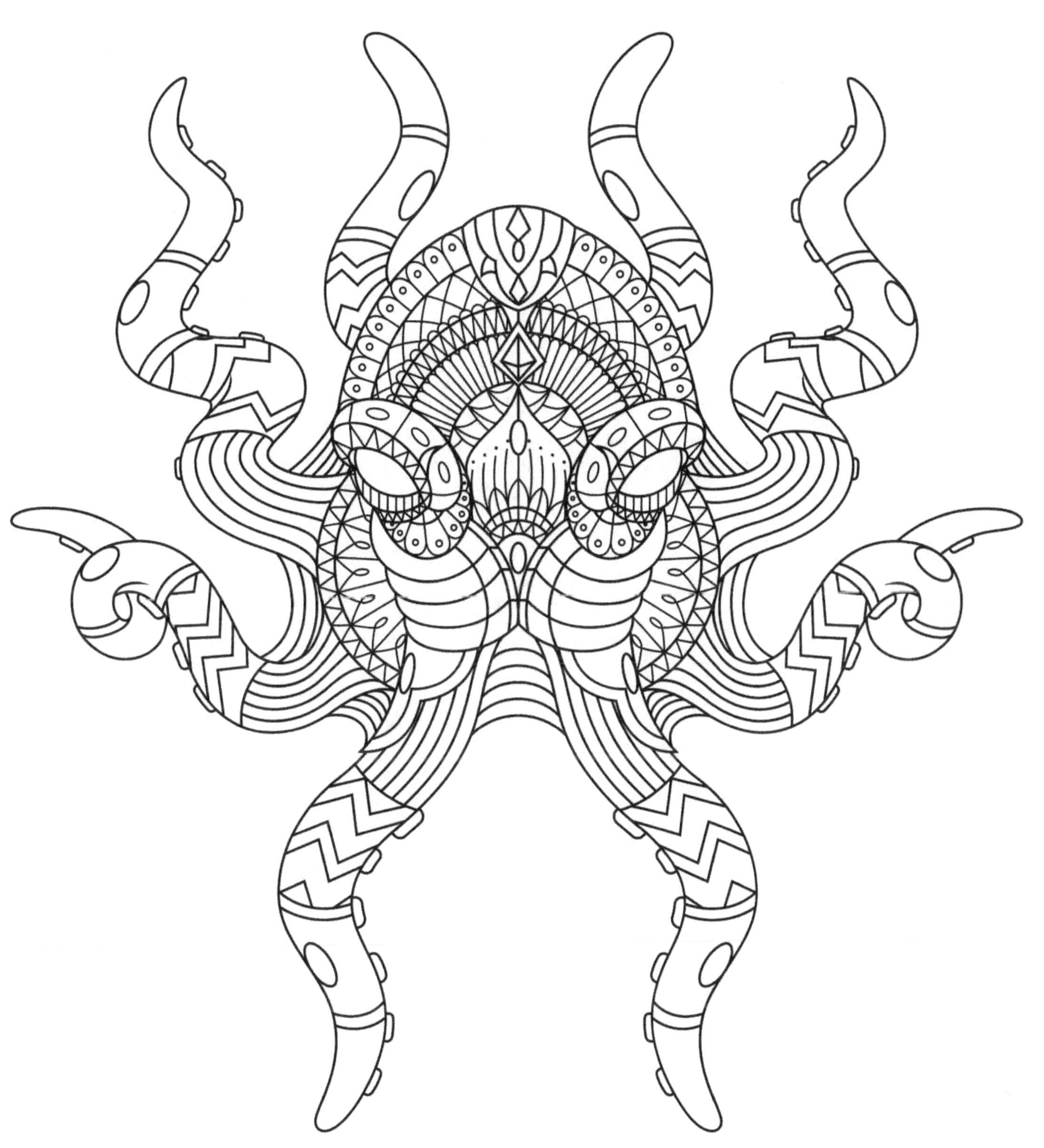

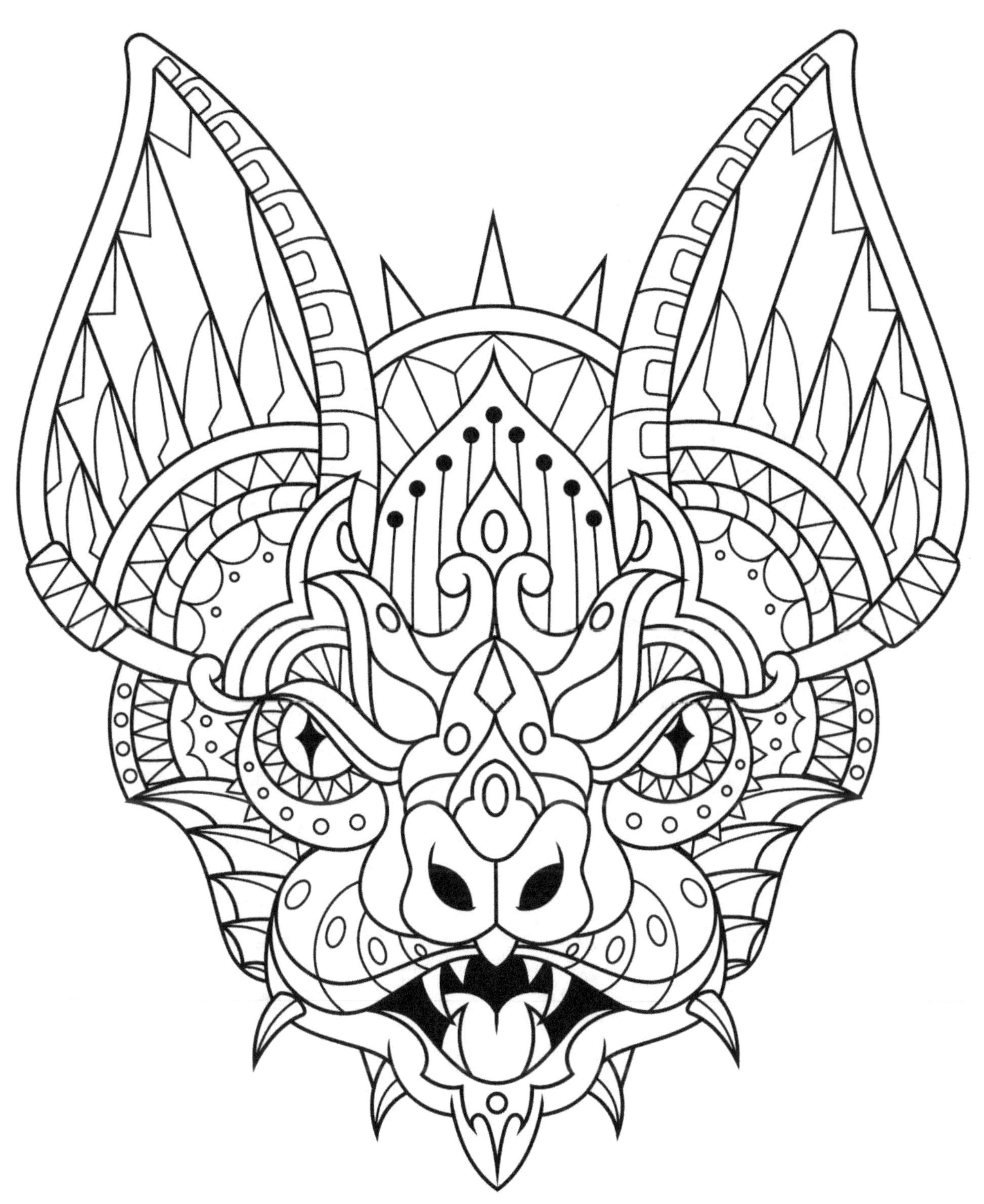

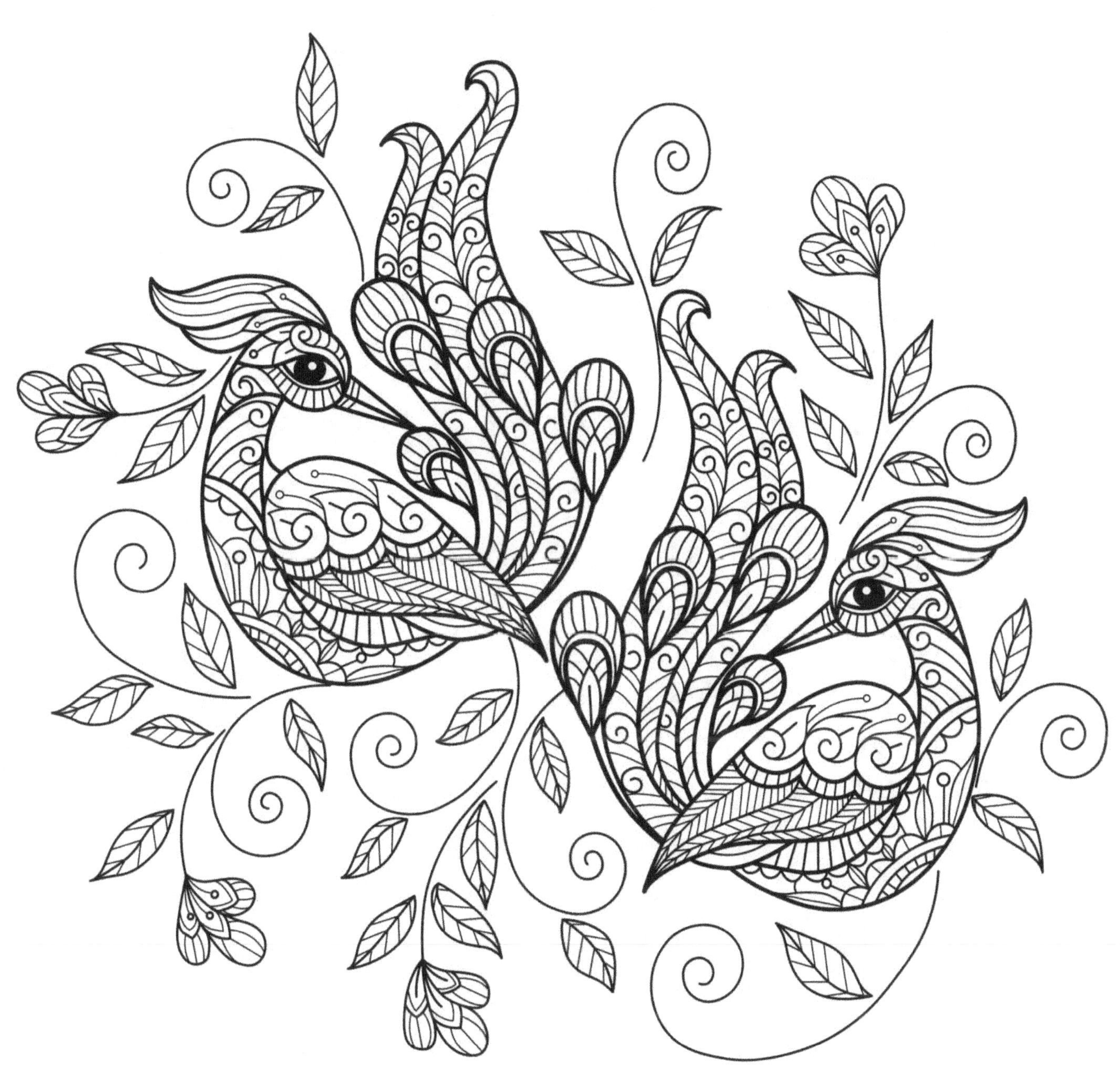

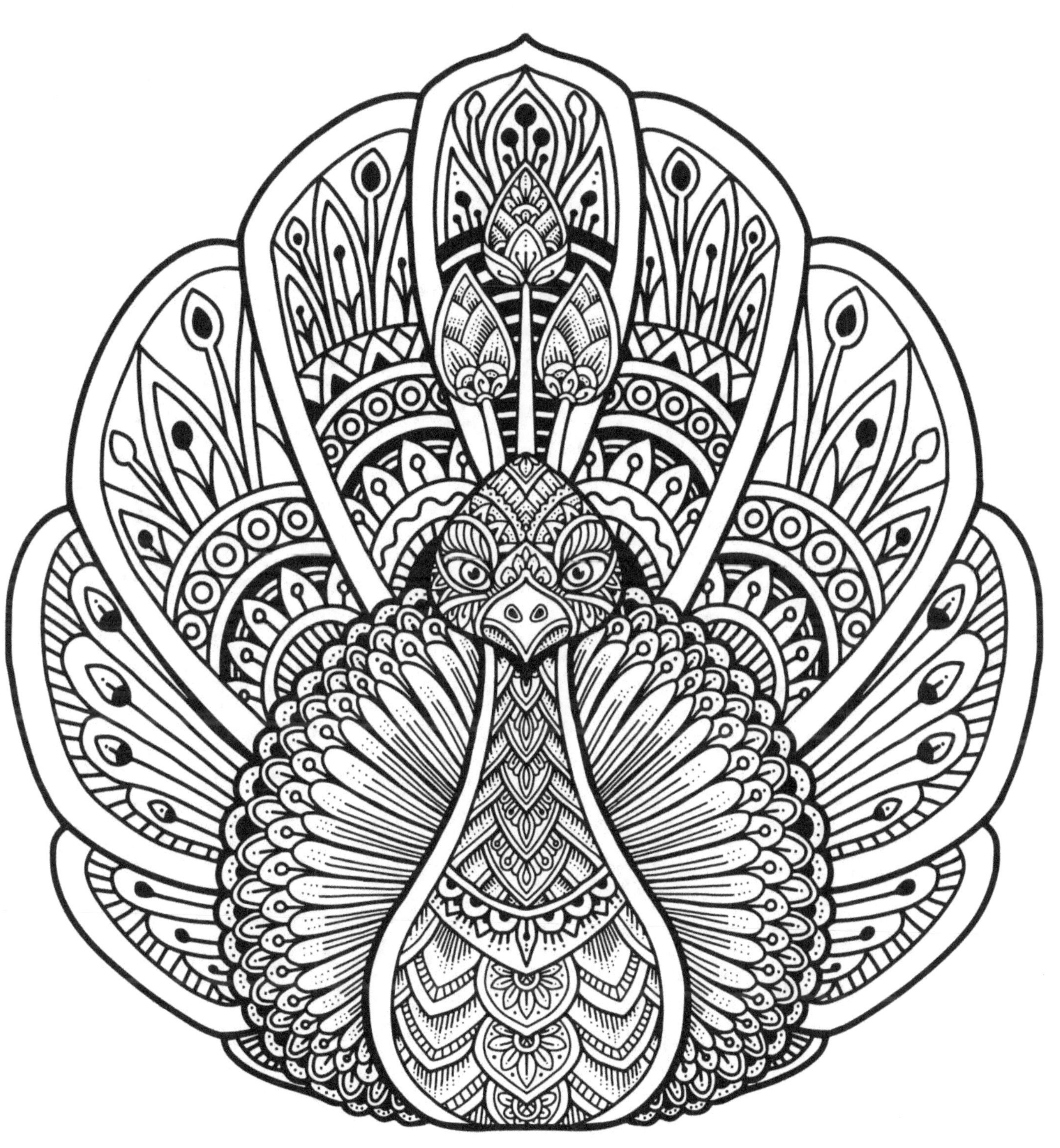

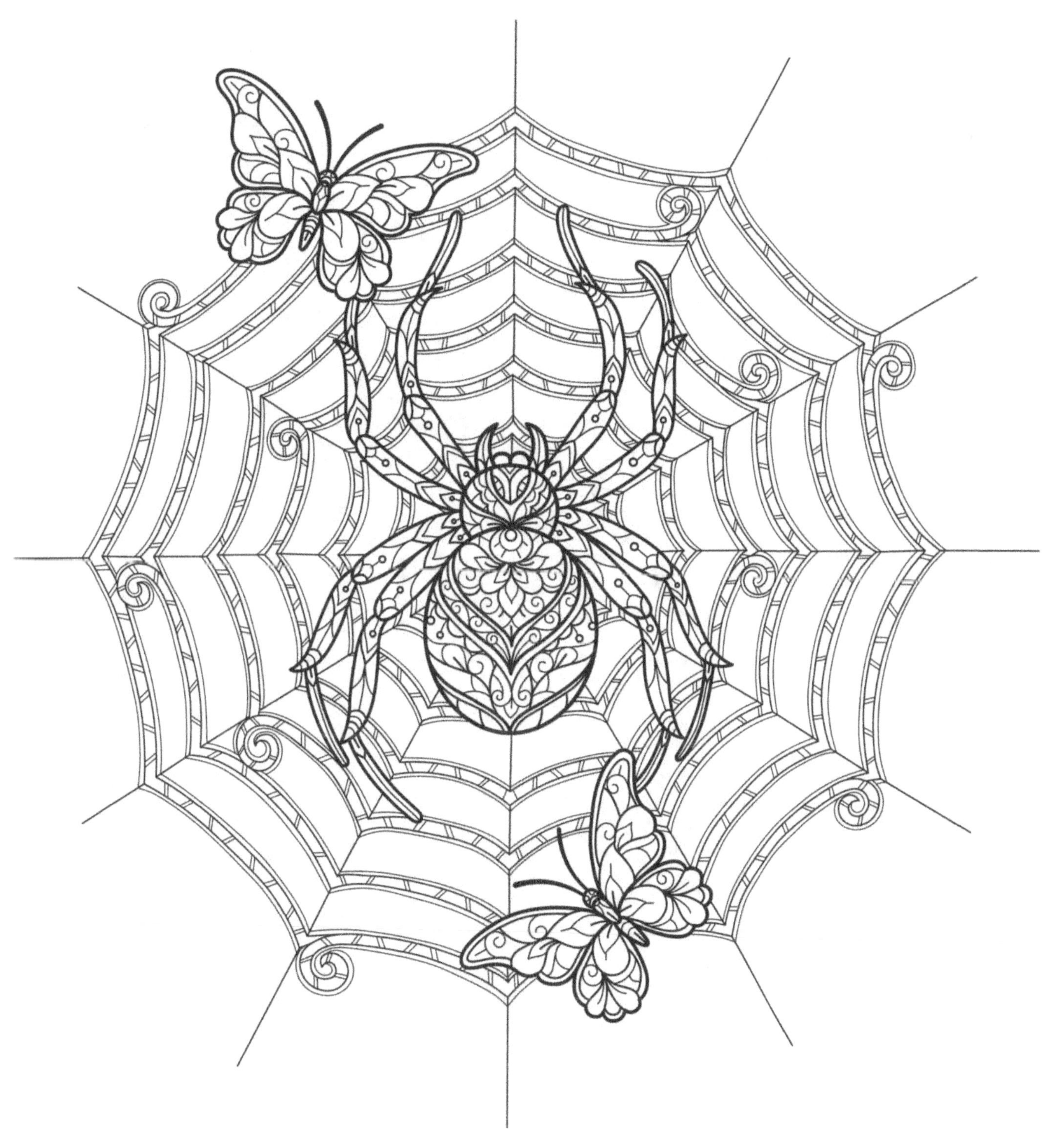

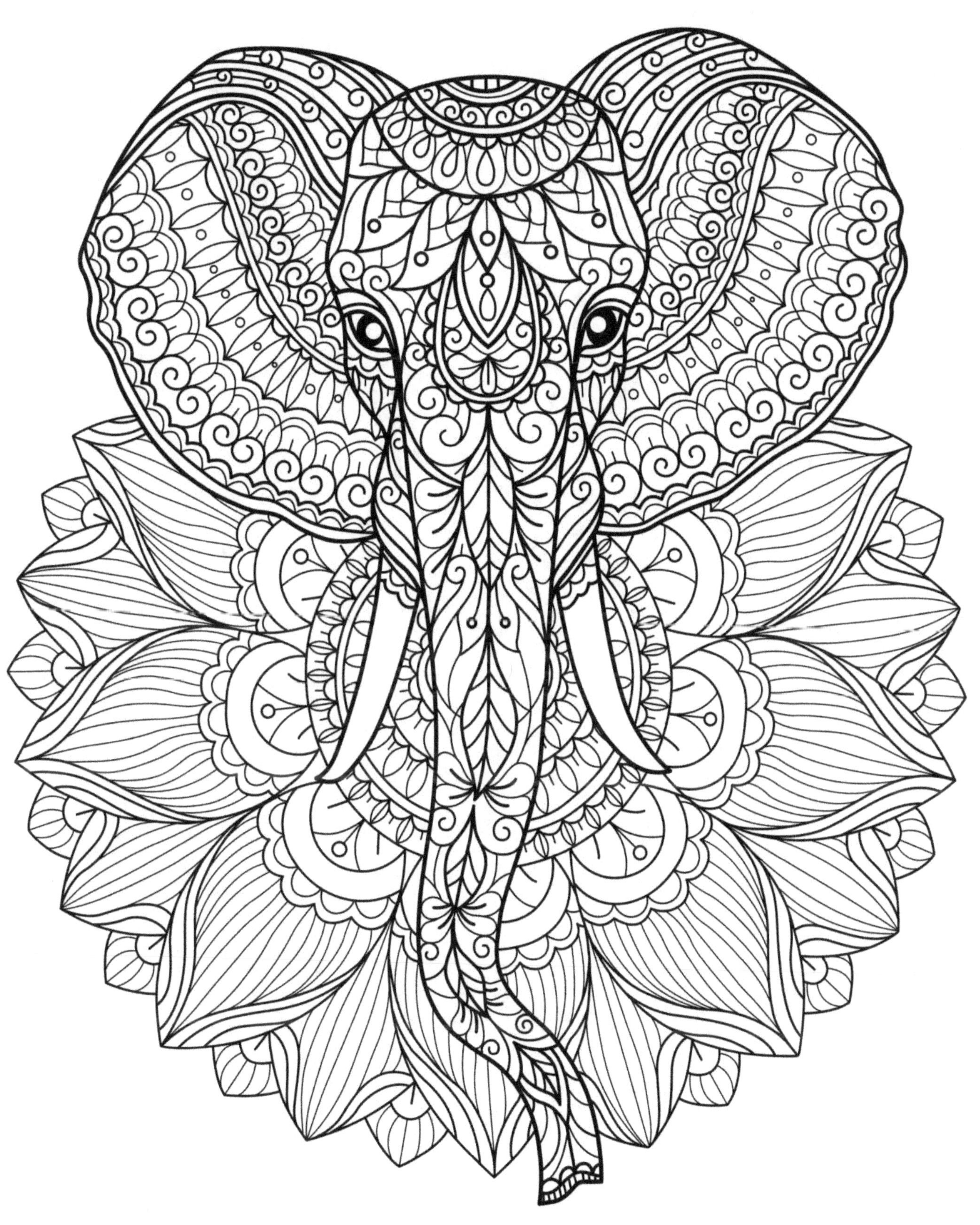

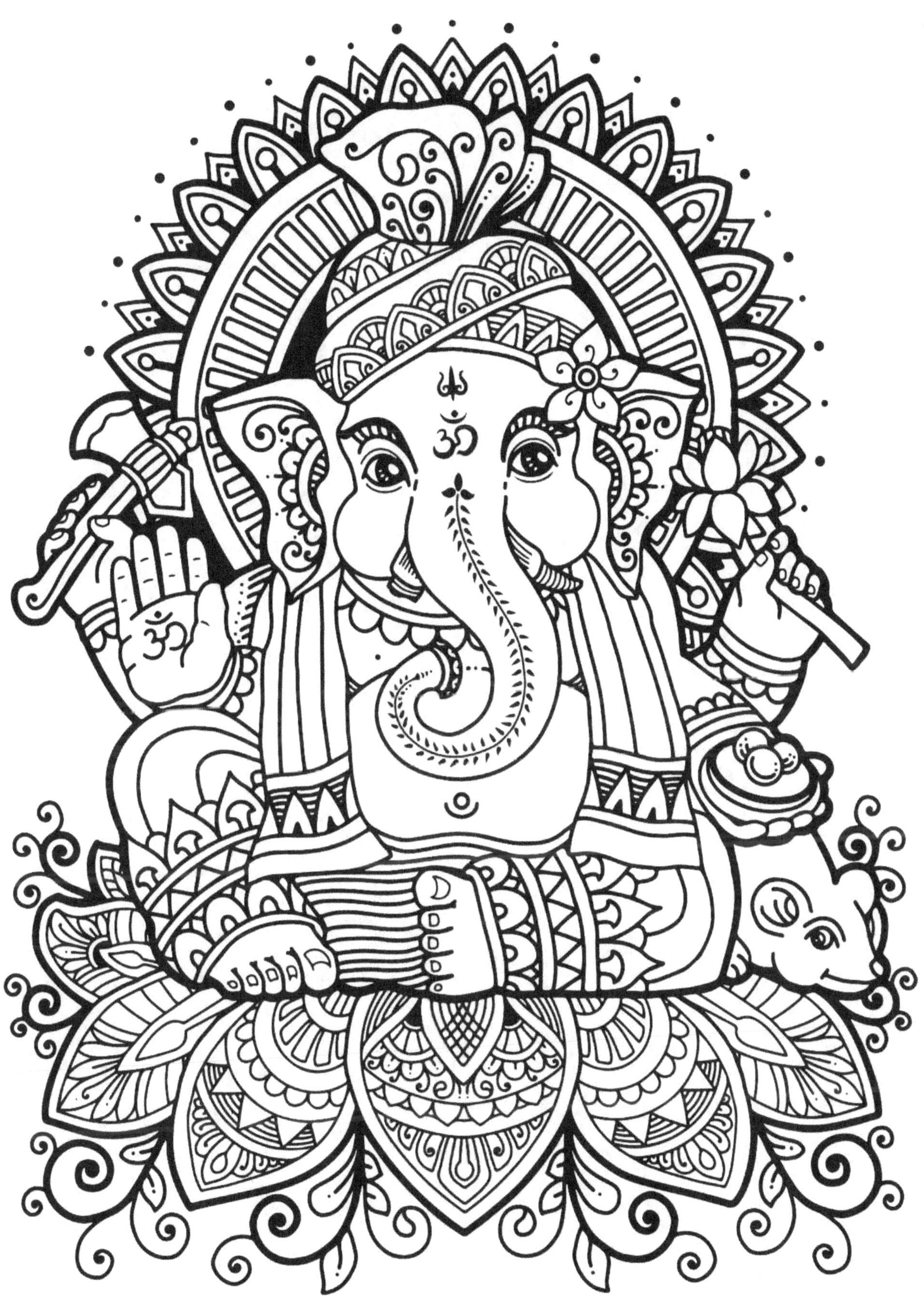

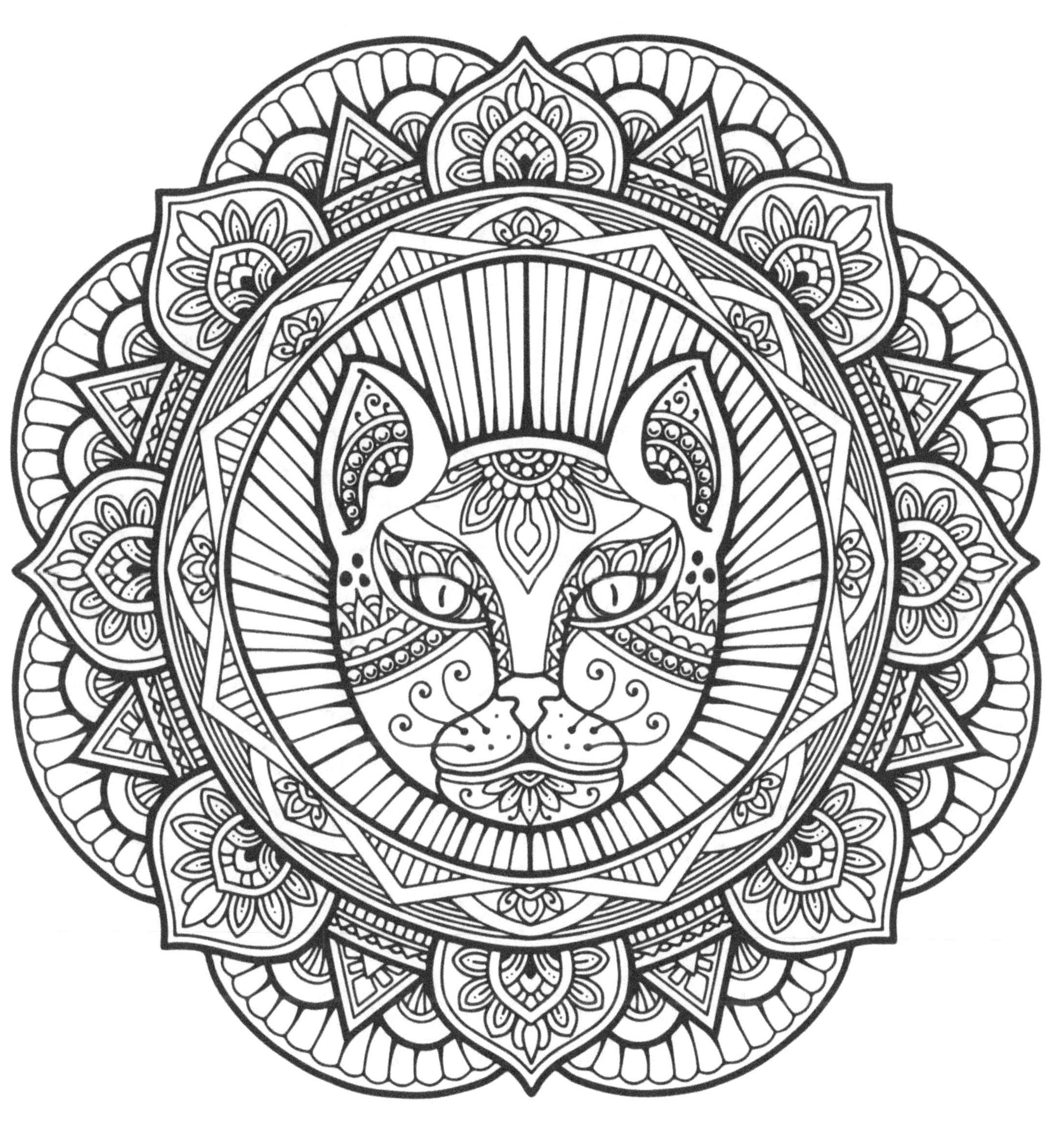

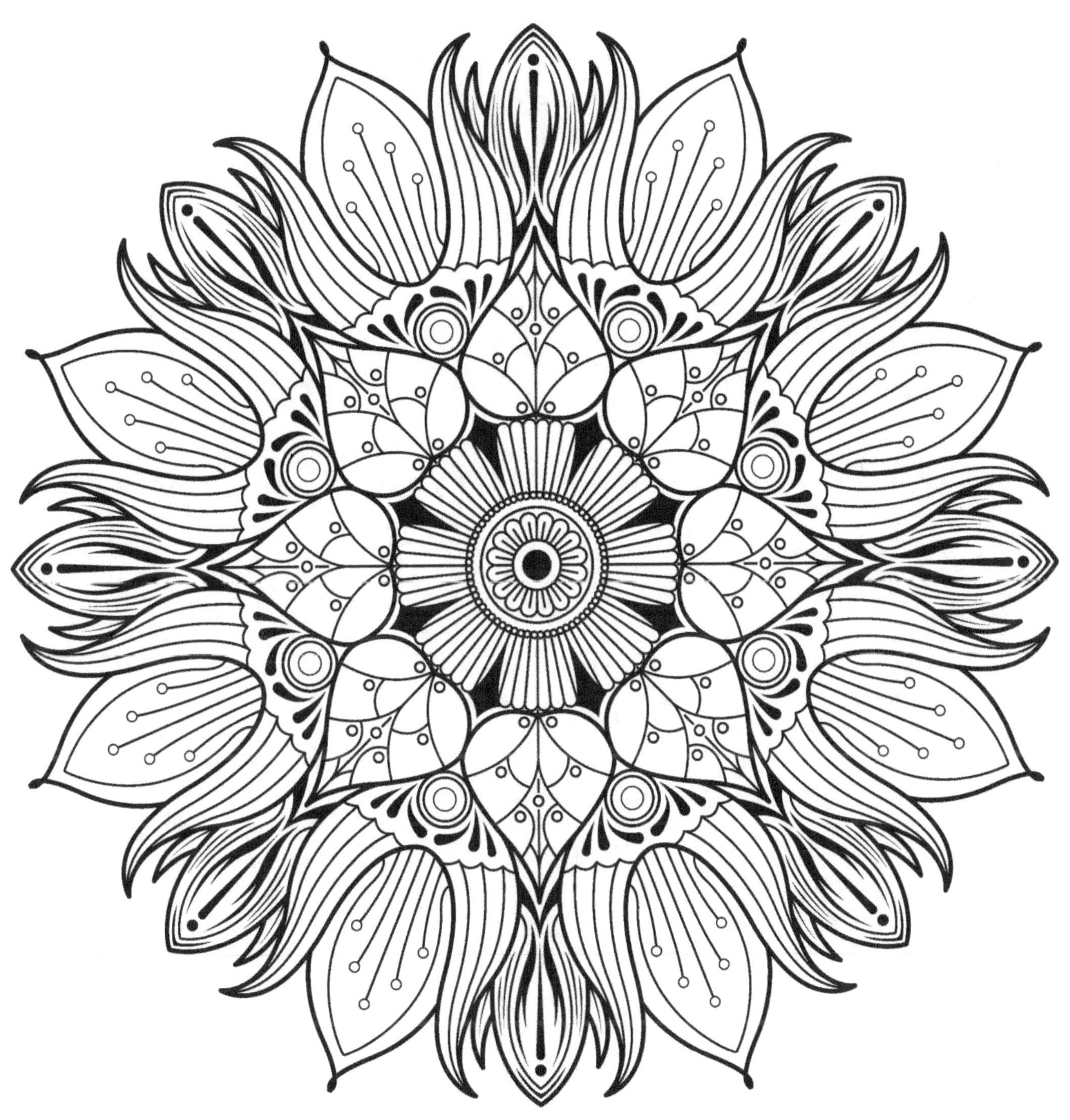

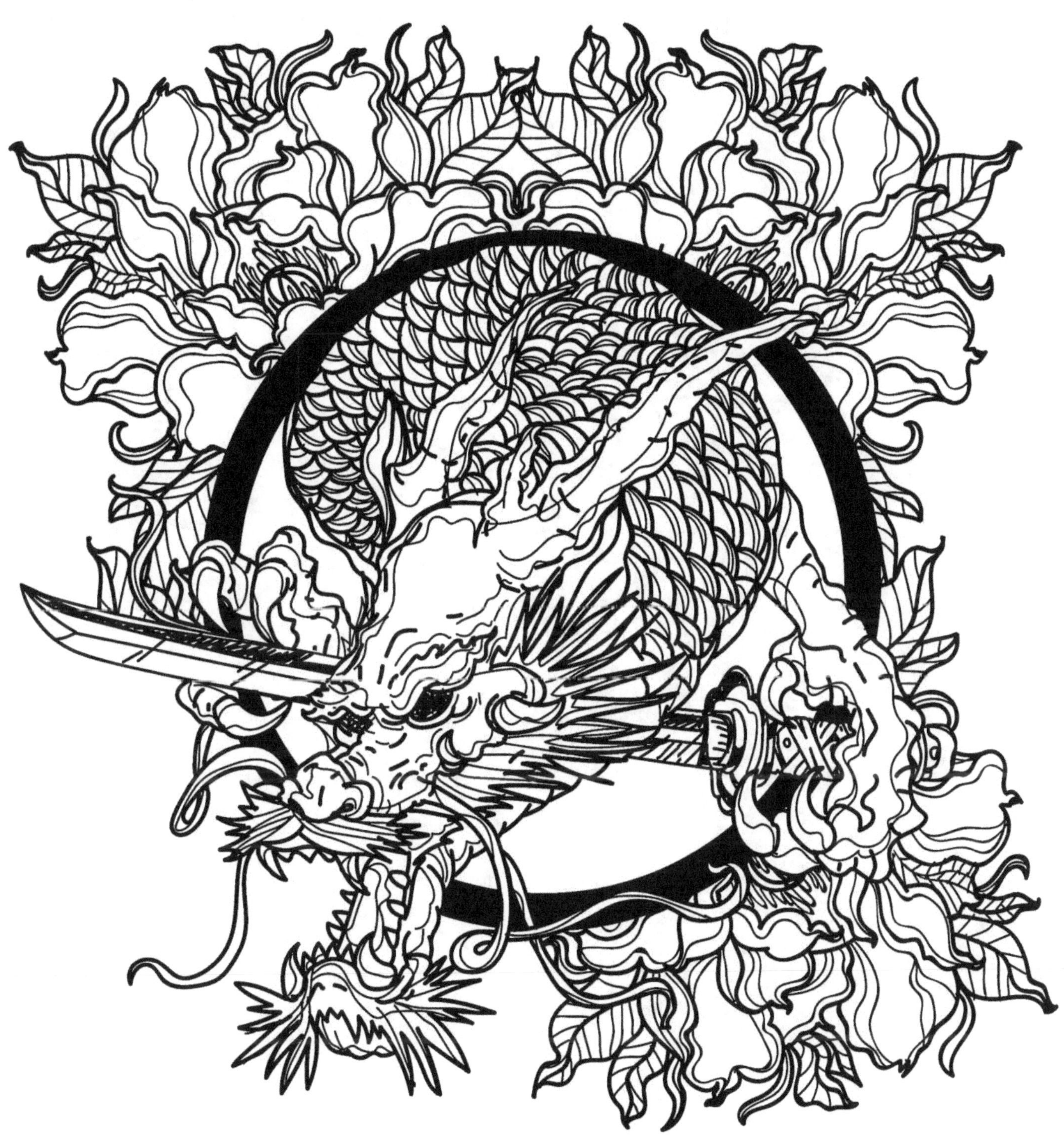

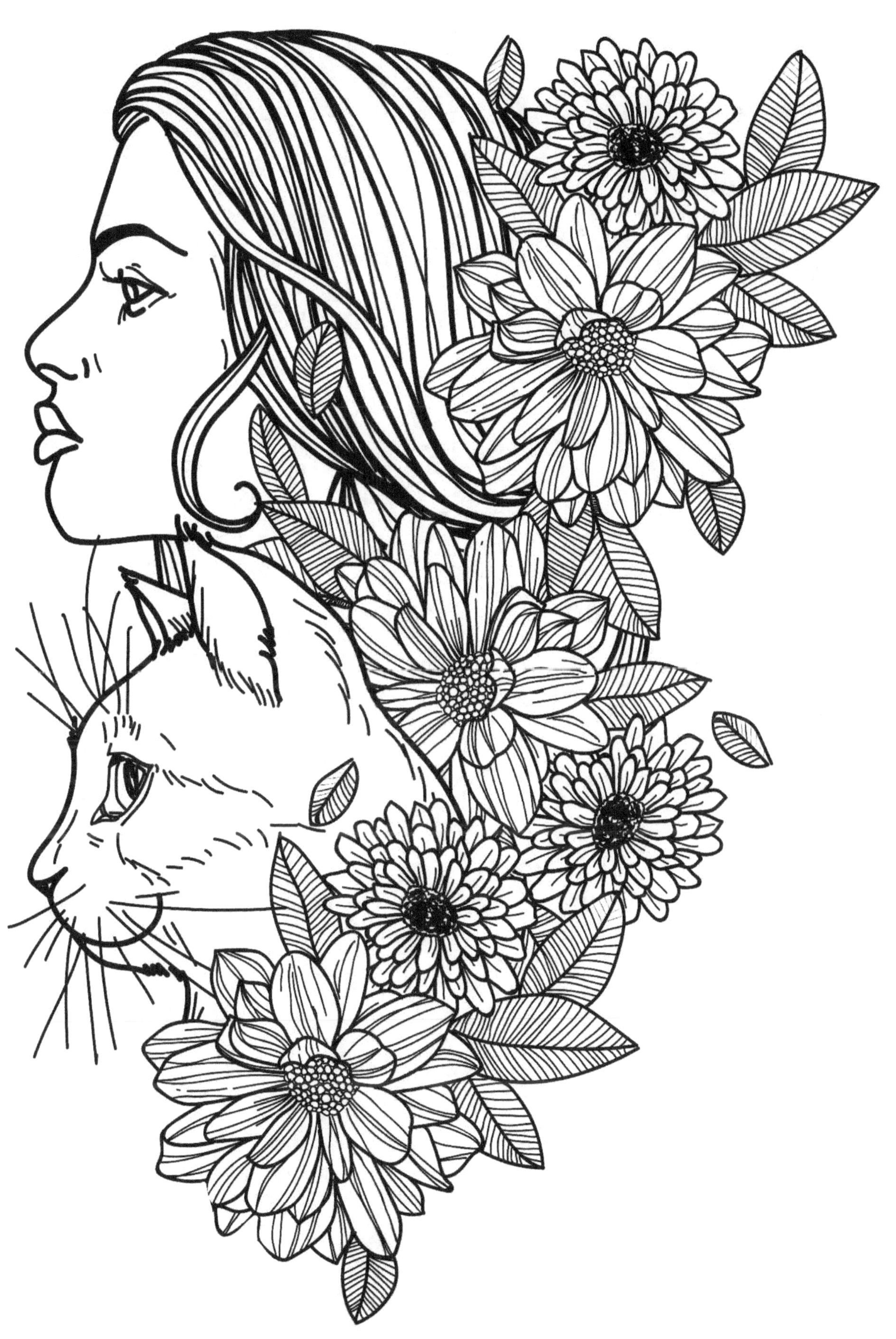

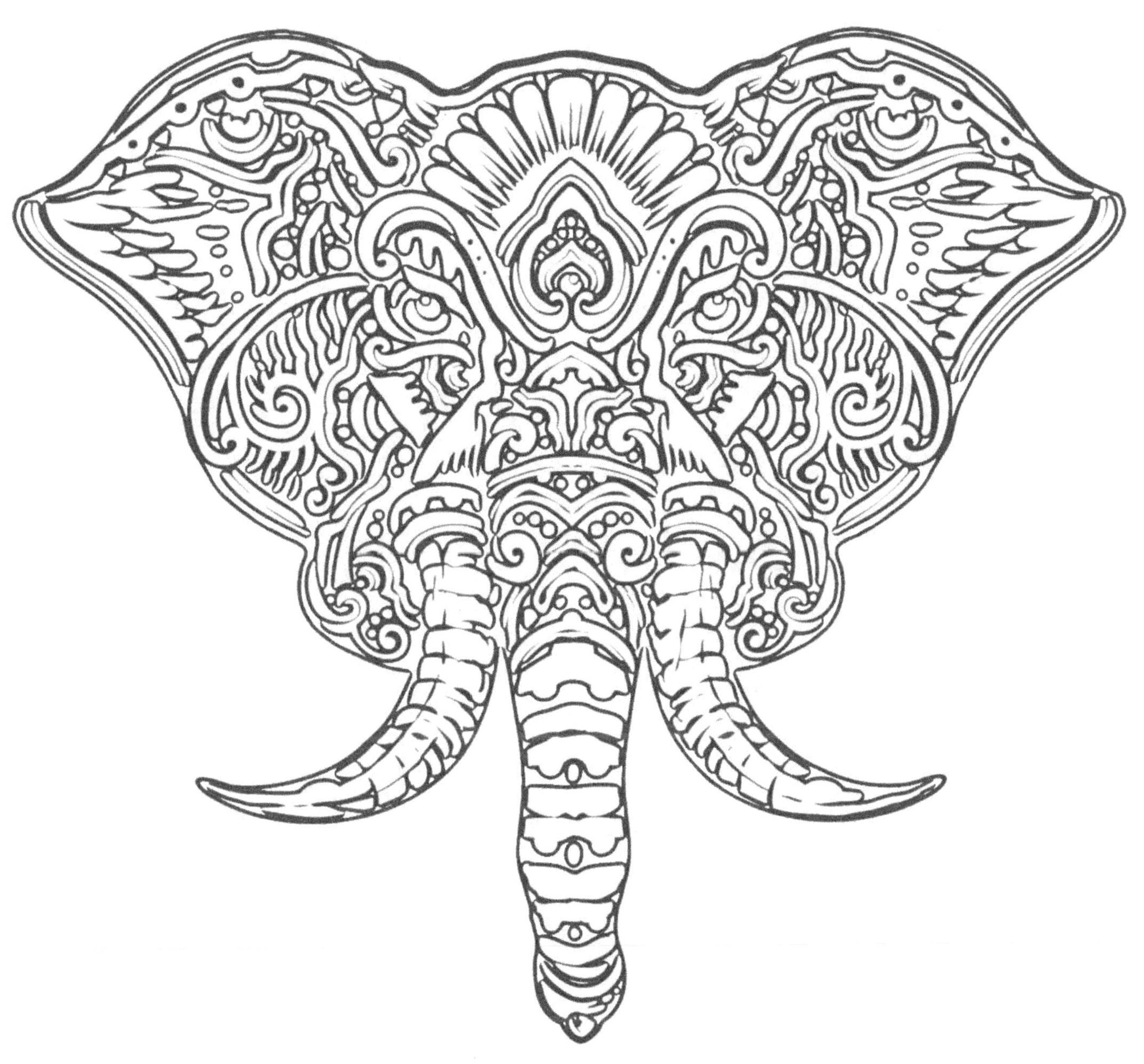

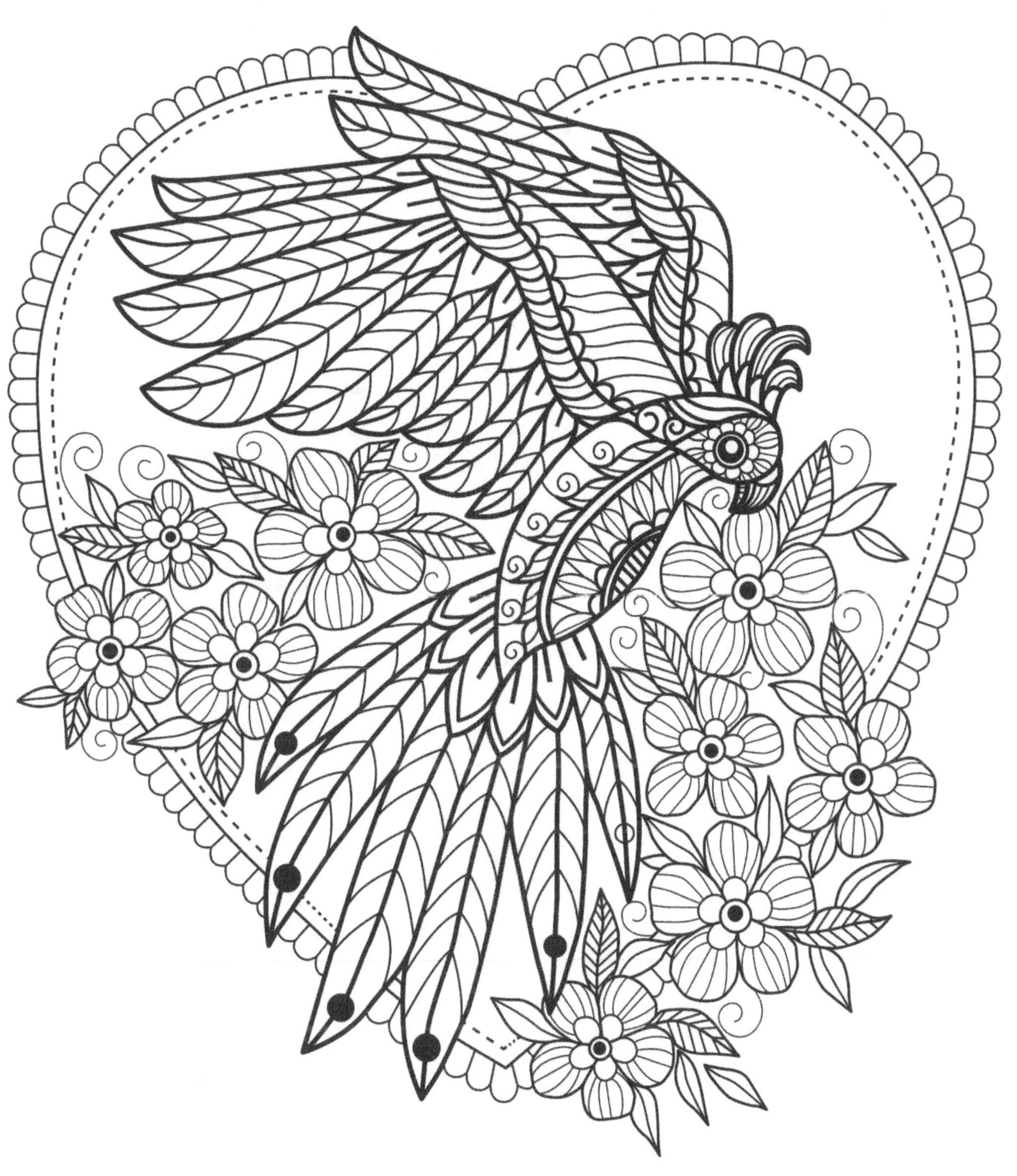

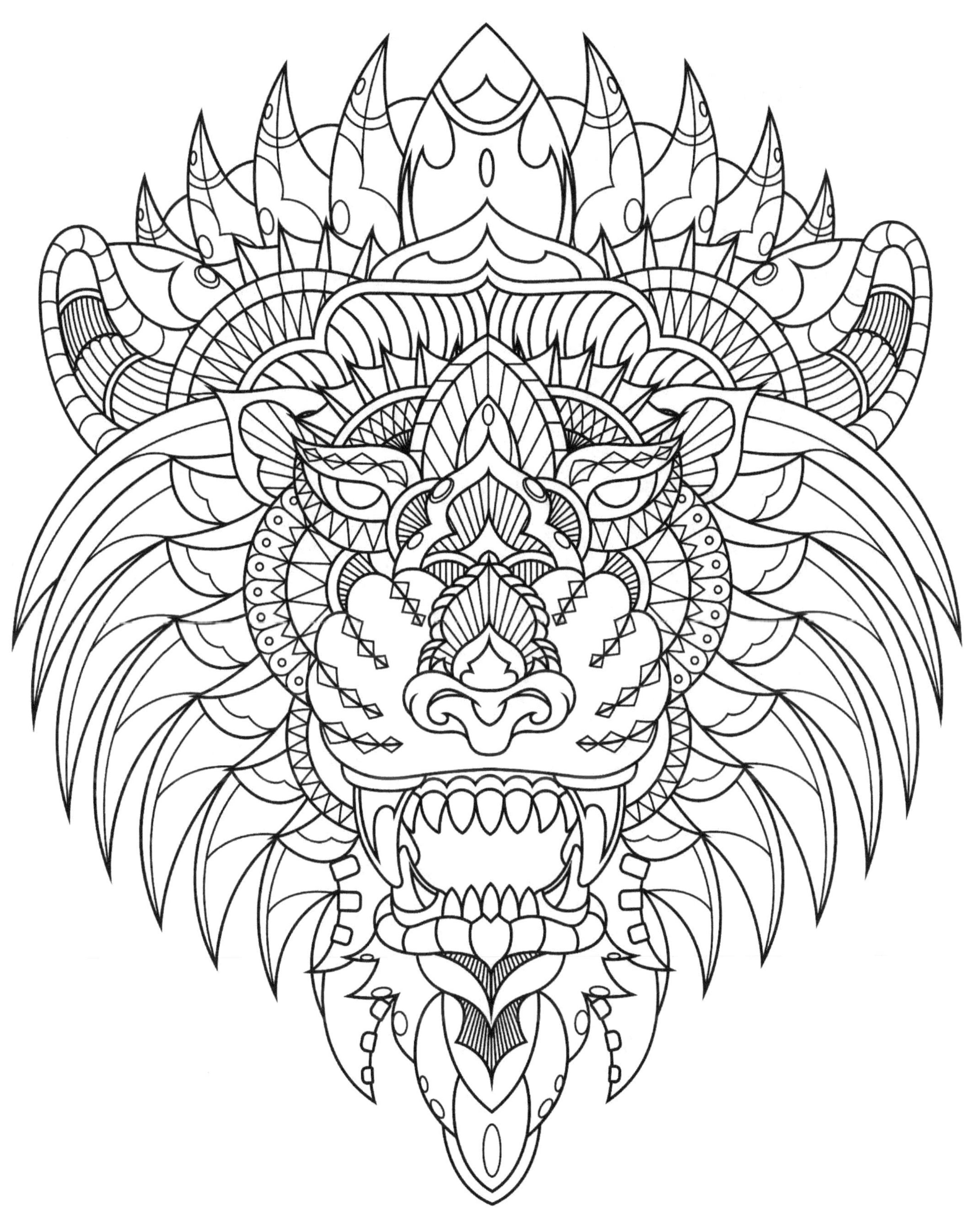

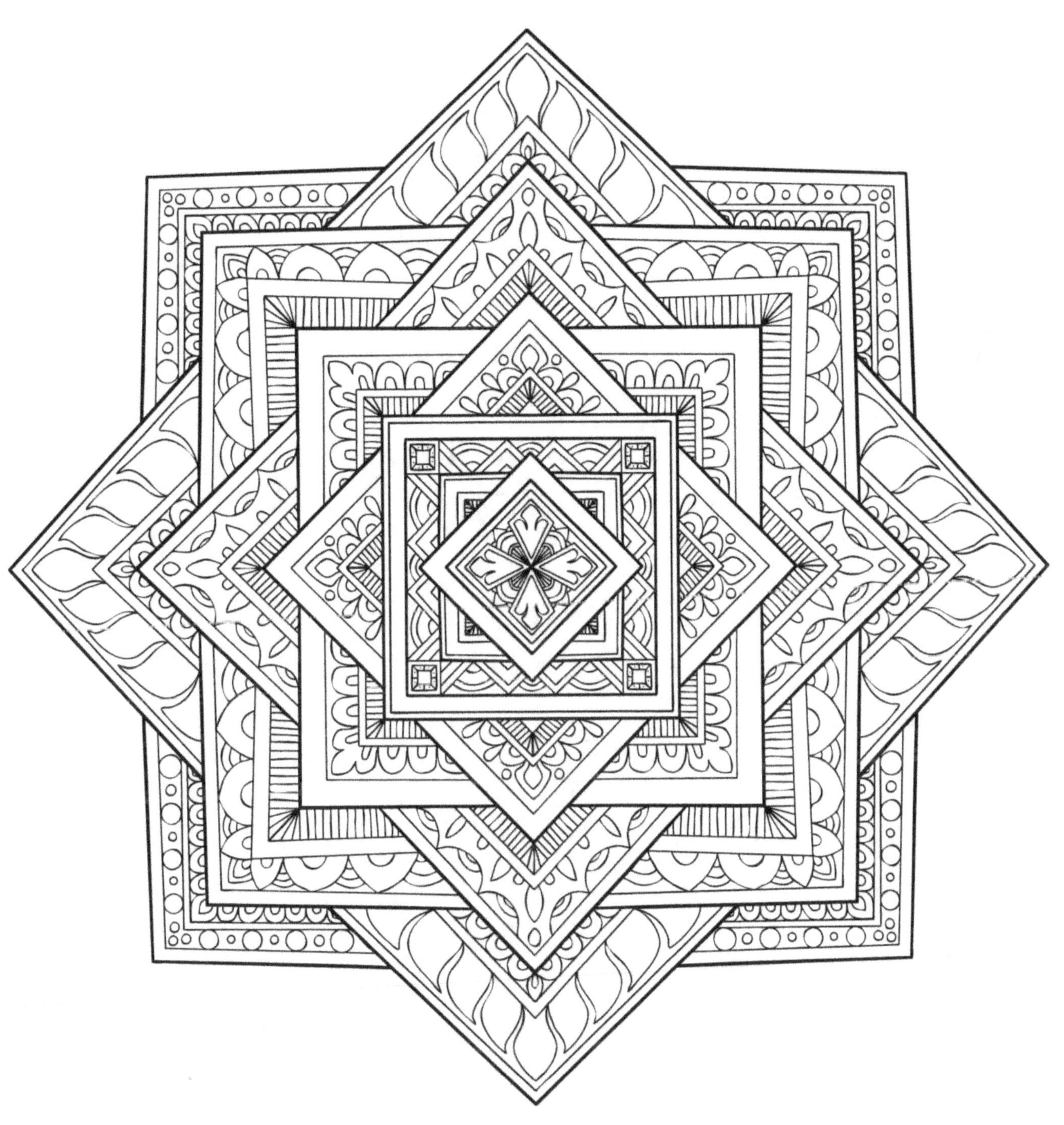

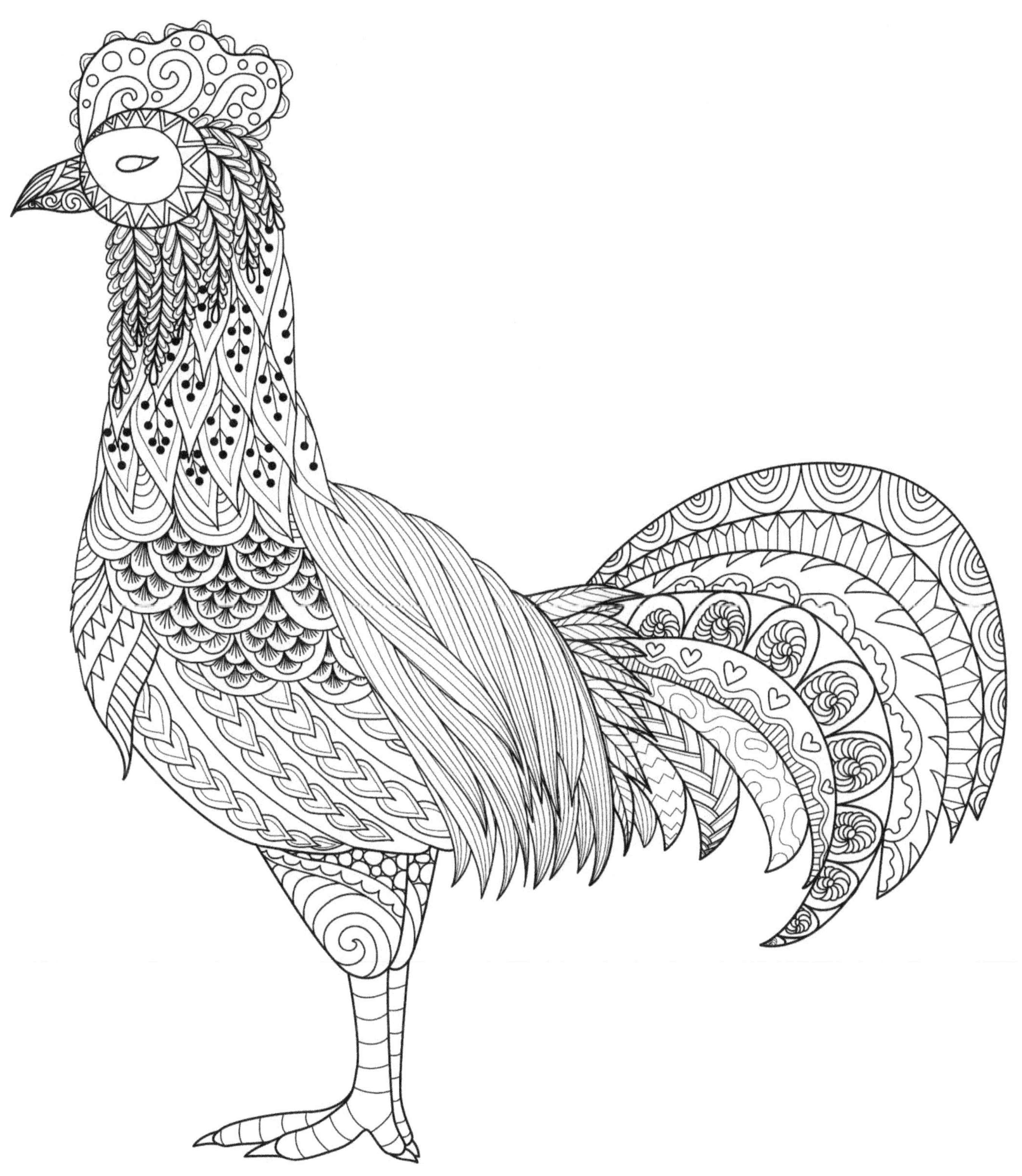

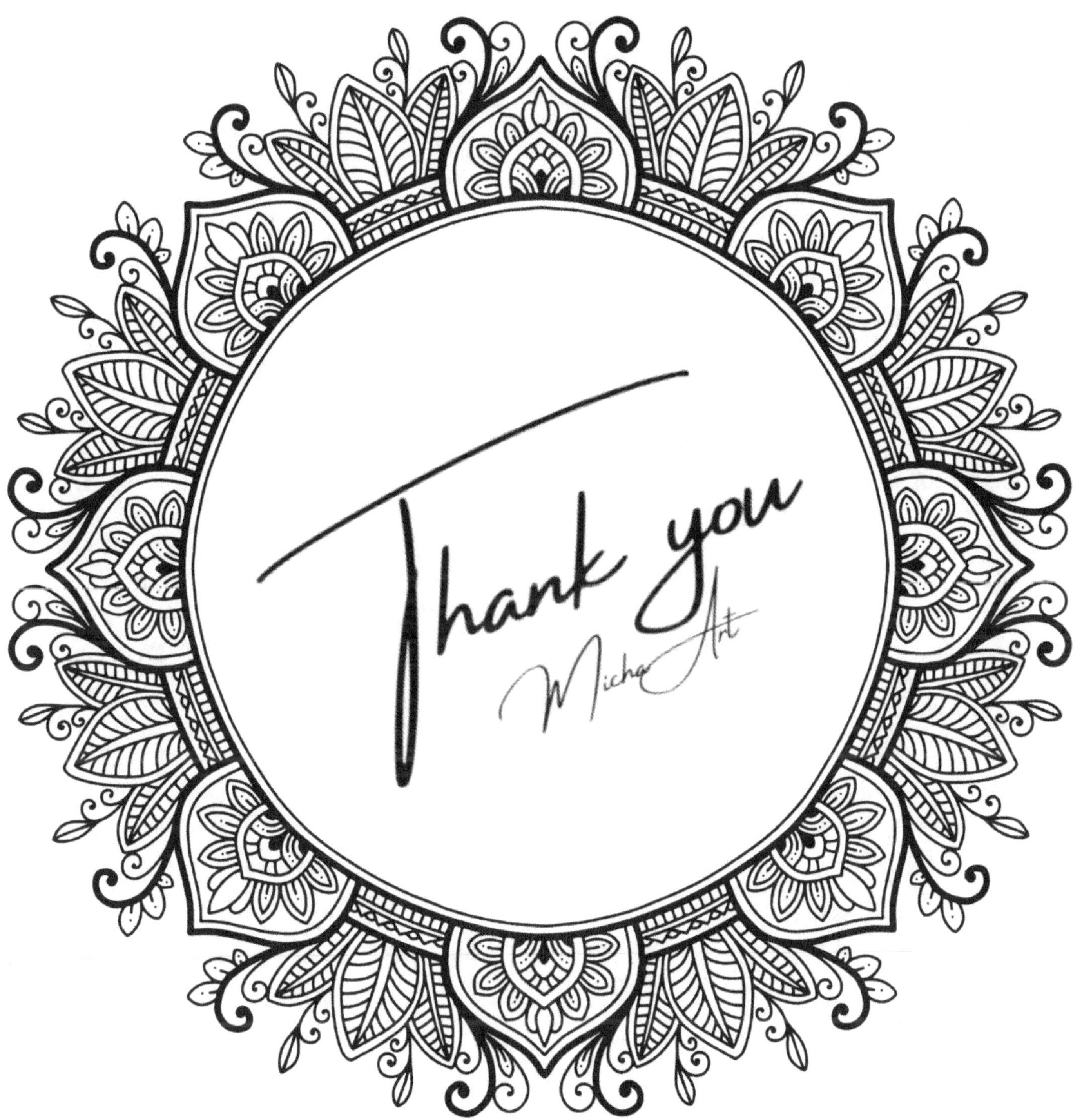

Thank you
Micha Art

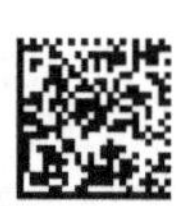
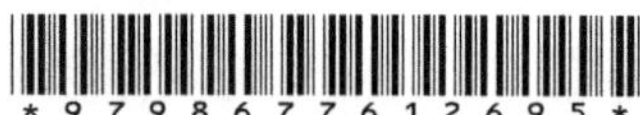